THE PEARL OF THE SOUTH

A BRIEF HISTORY

Chapter 1

›ber of 1492, three vessels sailed past a
erspersed with pale, sandy beaches. Bright
shed onto the beach in cascading waves.
ps crept past thick mangroves and into an
it would turn into an inland river. Their
lore, stop, and gather supplies for a long
the Atlantic Ocean.

were named *La Niña, La Pinta, and La Santa*

Christopher Columbus, was in awe of the
He called it, "The most beautiful island
ever seen."

s struggles for independence in 1868 with
War that ended in Spain's favor. In 1895,
naries did not give up, and war broke out
ops. Years later, the United States became
war when one of its battleships, The *USS*

RESCUED BY THE LIGHT

By

Helena Kemper

Blessings! Joshua 1:9 Helena Kemper 2020

Cover Design by Elizabeth Pease.

Interior Design by Caleb Wygal.

First printing, 2020.

Some names have been changed to protect privacy.

Since the Spaniards were suspected of sabotage, a brief Spanish-American war erupted, with Americans and Cuban forces fighting together, prevailing over the Spanish. The United States gained control of Cuba with the treaty of Paris and, in 1902, gave Cuba its independence.

When the war ended, many Spaniards, including my mother's descendants, remained in Cuba even though it was no longer a province of their homeland.

The United States occupied Cuba with a promise that it would grant sovereignty and its own government. Within the next four years, American companies invested in the Cuban economy, such as in sugar and tobacco plants. Public health and schools proliferated in the country.

Eventually, the Cuban people established a constitution, setting up a republican form of government with individual rights and liberties. The United States began withdrawing troops, but they prohibited Cuba from transferring land to other countries or entering any foreign treaties that would undermine Cuba's independence. The United States maintained the right to intervene militarily in Cuba's soil if the United States' interests or citizens were being threatened.

Political parties were created, and elections were set in dozens of Cuban cities. In 1902, Tomàs Estrada Palma was elected president. Keeping strong leadership became a problem soon after Cuba gained its independence.

The regime of President Palma collapsed in 1906, which resulted in four more years of Americans' occupation maintaining civil peace and protecting American interests. However, three years later American troops withdrew after Cuba had stabilized.

Over the next 27 years, four presidents served Cuba, but the political upheavals continued.

Gerardo Machado was a popular president in his first term of office. Unfortunately, problems started when he bypassed the constitution by seeking re-election to a second term.

In 1929 when the Great Depression began, Machado was forced to reduce salaries of public employees, creating discord, strikes, and violence among the workers.

In 1930, Machado closed the University of Havana, the site of protests to his regime. By now, hundreds of thousands had been unemployed. President Machado became a dictator who met growing resistance before being forced out of Cuba in 1933.

The Provisional Revolutionary Government was a new coalition, led by a university professor, Ramòn Grau San Martìn, who took brief control after Machado was gone. During this period, new freedoms came to Cuba, including an eight-hour workday, the minimum wage for sugarcane workers, and women gained the right to vote.

Many advanced social reforms in the constitution were very progressive for its time, such as social security, workplace rules, individuals' rights, and prohibitions of discrimination. Cuba was a sophisticated country. It had a large middle class with a high capita income, along with an excellent healthcare system—the best in Latin America.

Hotels, bars, and casinos in Havana, Cuba offered a picture of glamour and allure that was played up by the press and promoters. With Cuba's natural beauty, it attracted many American businesses and tourists.

Unfortunately, Cuba's charm also attracted criminal

organizations that caused chaos in different ways. These mobs didn't represent the strong family values of the Cuban people.

In 1934, Fulgencio Batista brought President Machado down by staging a successful coup. He became the unofficial leader of Cuba until 1940. He was later elected President of Cuba from 1940-1944. Eventually, Batista moved to the United States, but returned to Cuba in 1952.

He then ran for President once again. Given little chance to win, he launched a military coup from the existing president, Carlos Prìo Socarràs, a few months before the scheduled presidential election.

As a fragile republic, Cuba attempted to strengthen, but mounting political radicalization and social strife climaxed in the dictatorship of Fulgencio Batista.

Batista became a strong-armed leader and took control of the press, curtailing the political activism of students and others. Salaries of working people climbed and the country's economy accelerated, with people now having money to spend. However, along with this came gambling, organized mafia, and corruption.

Violent protests against Batista broke out at the University of Havana, and opposition to his corrupt and repressive regime grew among political, religious, businesses, and educational factions.

Fidel Castro, who was born in Cuba, educated by Jesuits priests and who later studied law at the University of Havana, organized armed forces attempting to overthrow Fulgencio Batista in 1952.

On July 26, 1953, Castro and a group of revolutionaries attacked The Moncada Barracks, a military post in Santiago de Cuba. The attempt failed, and Castro was tried and sent to prison. However, in 1955, he was freed as part of a widespread amnesty bill that had passed that year in Cuba's congress. This date of July 26 gave way to the July 26 Movement.

After Fidel Castro was freed, he exiled to Mexico. While there, he joined forces with Argentine Ernesto "Che" Guevara. He was responsible for many unnecessary horrific crimes during the Revolution.

In December 1956, Fidel Castro and many other insurgents, including Camilo Cienfuegos, Che Guevara, Castro's brother Raùl, and Juan Almeida Bosque, returned to Cuba in a boat called *Granma.*

Castro and the other men had plans to disembark in a part of the larger Oriente province. They had chosen the location to emulate the voyage of national hero, Josè Martì, who had landed in the same region sixty-one years earlier during the wars for independence from Spanish Colonial rule.

They intended to overthrow Batista's regime once again. However, Batista's forces were waiting for them. The rebels forced the ship at a spot called *Playa de las Coloradas*, about fifteen miles south of the designated place.

The new landing area was more of a muddy swamp. For this reason, the rebels were unable to unload most of their weapons.

Many of Castro's men were killed or imprisoned, except for himself and others who were able to escape to the *Sierra Maestra* Mountains. Castro's plan derailed and was unsuccessful for the time being.

I grew up in the province of Camaguey, fifty miles from

where Columbus had his first up-close look of the island.

Over the centuries following its discovery, the island retained its allure as England, Spain, and France fought for its possession. Political upheaval has been a common theme throughout Cuba's history. However, the physical landscape there still retains much of the majesty that drew those words from Columbus. The political landscape is the antithesis of that and has been for many years.

I was there when Fidel Castro rose to power. I was there when Communism swept through the nation. I was there and experienced many of the horrific events and tragedies that befell the people of Cuba. *This is my story.*

MY FATHER

Chapter 2

My father always wore a suit.

I never knew my paternal grandmother, Josefa, but my father *Arnaldo Cebriàn de Quesada* told me she died giving birth to her last child, Amanda. Including my father, there were nine siblings.

After the death of my paternal grandmother, matters changed in my young father's life. His father, Adalberto, hired a friend of the family, named Antonia, to care for all nine children. My father, who was very fond of Antonia, learned many things from her. In her, my father always found a shoulder to cry on when life got tough. The absence of his mother was, at times, unbearable. However, as a young boy, he remembered the one thing his mother had always told him. "Arnaldo, when you feel lost or lonely, always pray The Lord's Prayer."

While Antonia took care of my dad and his siblings, my grandfather came home less and less. The lack of interaction with his children quickly affected his relationship with his family. The youngest child, Amanda, who was still a baby, needed much more attention than Antonia could give her. One evening, after a very exhausting day, Antonia told Adalberto she had enough of his absence. She packed her bags and walked out the door.

Not long after Antonia had left, my grandfather moved Maria into their home, a woman he had seen for quite some time following the death of my grandmother. My father said she was a strange woman and difficult to get along with.

She was mean to the children and did not treat my grandfather well. However, Adalberto seemed blinded by the artificial love she portrayed in front of him and his children.

My father soon rebelled against Maria's authority, sensing that this woman did not have good intentions with his father.

Infuriated by my father's rebellion, Adalberto distributed all his children to other family members so that he could continue his relationship in peace with Maria.

My grandfather sent the girls to stay with their aunts, but the boys weren't so lucky. He sent them out on the streets to fend for themselves. At only ten years old and with little education, my father's journey was full of trials and struggles.

Fortunately for him, between his maternal grandmother and Antonia, he sometimes had a place where he could sleep and have a warm meal.

At the tender age of eleven, my father got his first job at a pharmacy as a delivery boy. Arnaldo learned to be a very hard worker throughout his childhood, which served him well as he got older. Santos, his boss, whose name ironically translated to "the saint", was a grumpy elderly man. Santos was always in a perpetual nasty mood.

No matter how hard my father worked, his labor went unnoticed. His boss would constantly yell at him, "Hurry up, Arnaldo! Clean up the floors!"

There were times Santos would slap my father on the back of his head, almost knocking him to the ground. He would accuse my father of not doing a good enough job. However, my father tolerated Santos' abuse, knowing that he had to keep his job so he could survive on his own.

Still grieving his mother, my father would spend many nights crying and reciting the Lord's Prayer. This prayer would console him, even if it were for just a little while. After two months of working at the pharmacy, he developed chickenpox. He stayed with his maternal grandmother, "Mamalola," until he recovered from his illness. After my father got well, he tried to go back to work, but Santos would not give my father his job back.

It was not long after my father lost his employment at the pharmacy, that he found a new job in a clothing store. His hard work paid off. He eventually began to earn fifteen dollars a month. Even though this was good in those days, he was still unable to save much money.

My father was very responsible as a child and he always made a point of helping his siblings out. Each month, three dollars went toward his night school, which he attended for a while. Six dollars went to help his impoverished maternal grandmother, three dollars went to help Hilda, his oldest sister, and the last three dollars he kept to buy his lunches.

Eventually, my father became the manager of the clothing store and started earning twenty-five dollars a month. Now he was able to save some money for the goals he had set for himself to become a journalist and a writer.

After years of working at the clothing store, my father decided that it was time for him to pursue his dreams and leave his past behind.

However, events took a unique turn in my father's life before he could reach his dreams. He worked at the Municipal Courts in Camaguey, Cuba. There he was engaged with persons of many political circles. Even though his dreams did not come into play until many years later, he did eventually publish several of his writings, along with a successful career as a television and radio newscaster.

FATHER FALLS IN LOVE

Chapter 3

My Parents when they met

During the 1940s, Cuba was the playground for the rich and famous. Much was going on during that time in our country, politically and culturally. An air of glamour and romance permeated throughout this charming island. It is no wonder that it was known as "The Pearl of the South."

As a young man, my father possessed dark olive skin, black hair, long eyelashes, and eyes that lit up when he smiled. That electric smile drove the Cuban ladies crazy!

Born and raised in the province of Camaguey, my dad, Arnaldo Cebrian de Quesada, earned the reputation of a ro-

My father working at CMJK Radio Station.

mantic bachelor.

My father was able to put himself through education as a journalist. His first career in his profession was at a radio station called *CMJW,* but his favorite job was at the *CMJK* in Camaguey. The show was called *La Voz del Camagueyano,* (The Voice of the Camagueyano). It was located on Republic Street near my godfather's, Jose Sabates, business. This street was one of the busiest and longest roads in Camaguey.

At the radio station, his coworkers would tease him about the romantic songs he sometimes played for the ladies in the listening audience— and this particular night was no different.

The year was 1944. As Arnaldo sat in his chair directing his voice into the oversized microphone, a young woman called in to request an American song.

"Hi, my name is *Sarah*. I would like to know if you could play a song called 'Fascination'?"

Being the hopeless romantic he was, he replied, "Of course, I'll play the song for you."

As he listened to the song Sarah requested, he daydreamed of meeting this young lady.

In early January, my father had an assignment to promote a raffle for the newspaper company where he sometimes enjoyed freelancing as a publicist.

The street in Camaguey where CJMK was located.

The winner of the raffle was Sarah- the same young woman that had called and requested that beautiful song, "Fascination."

Immediately, he volunteered to deliver the prize personally, intending to meet this mystery lady. When he arrived at her home, he nervously knocked on the large wooden door.

Sarah opened the door and said, "May I help you?"

My father's life had been an adventurous one up to that point. He was quite the ladies' man. For this reason, he wasn't too sure that he wanted to give Sarah an answer to her question.

He told me that, at that very moment, he was unsure whether he should run or stay. He said that the beauty that Sarah possessed might forever change the course of his life.

Despite his awkwardness, Arnaldo's eyes met Sarah's captivating green ones. The sun's rays shone through Sarah's shoulder-length blonde hair, giving her an almost heavenly glow. He thought she was the most beautiful woman he had ever laid eyes on.

Sarah interrupted his dumbfounded expression and said, "Sir, may I help you?"

He snapped out of his trance and made his move.

Slowing his steps towards Sarah, he took in every detail of her beauty. He blinked twice to make sure she was real and then said, "I am here to deliver your prize from the raffle you had entered a while ago."

In an almost childlike way, Sarah jumped up and down with excitement. She leaned over and gave Arnaldo a great enormous hug as she thanked him over and over.

After the awkward encounter he had with Sarah, he paid her another visit later that week. This time, he was not about to hold back on getting to know her. He charmed Sarah into spending the rest of her life with him.

They married on June 8, 1944.

Shortly after their romantic honeymoon in Varadero Beach, he built her the house of her dreams. Despite humble beginnings, my father became successful in his career. He could now grant her wish.

Our house was on a large corner lot in a neighborhood called Reparto Bobes. A beautiful garden surrounded the pale green stucco house. Roses, gladiolus, and other flowers kept my mother occupied for hours as she tended them. An enormous evergreen tree in front of our home was breathtaking. A low stucco fence surrounded the front and side of the house. There was a concrete privacy fence in the back yard that served as a barrier from the streets.

The front door was glass with a cast-iron cutout of a man's face speaking into a microphone. It represented my father's profession. His new goal was to keep my mother happy. However, something was missing—a baby!

MOTHER GETS HER WISH

Chapter 4

MY MOTHER, SARAH DELGADO CEBRIAN

My mother, Sarah Delgado Roques, was the youngest of six children- four girls and two boys. My maternal grandfather was Quintin, and my maternal grandmother was Consuelo. I never knew them. Like my father, she became an orphan at two years old. After the death of her parents, her grandparents raised my mother and her siblings. They were extremely strict with them. Her upbringing was very dysfunctional, and the physical and psychological abuse she endured at home left her with many long-term emotional scars. Emma was the sibling she was closest to. They were inseparable. They also spent a lot of time in boarding schools at Las Salesianas Catholic school.

MY MOTHER AND I WHEN I WAS 4 YEARS OLD.

My mother was a sociable woman. She attended the Women's Rotary Club with the wives of my father's colleagues, and she loved to play cards with her friends. Canasta was her favorite. She taught herself how to play the piano, and eventually, my father surprised her with a beautiful cream color upright piano of her own. She always dressed in her finest, and her favorite perfume was Shalimar.

After being married for almost six years, the conversations of having a baby never ceased. My mother was born with a congenital heart defect, her doctor in Cuba had recommended against her getting pregnant, but despite the doctor's recommendation, mother insisted.

In the early 1950s, my parents decided to seek a physician in *Miami, Florida.* They went across the ocean, ninety miles from our beloved country, in search of a medical miracle—so I was told.

After doing some sightseeing in Florida, they went to talk to a doctor that specializes in heart disease. With the advancement of medical science, this doctor didn't think there would be a problem with my mother having a baby. Excited by the news from the doctor, they spent a few more days touring Miami, bought a television to take home, and then traveled back to Cuba hoping to become parents.

On May 20, 1954, I was born and named Helena. Or so the story goes!

ME AND MOM

CAMAGUEY MY CITY

Chapter 5

The city where I grew up has its personal history. Camaguey is a historic and beautiful city, one of the most populous in Cuba. Spanish Colonists found Camaguey around 1514, as the village of Santa Maria del Puerto del Principe, on the northern coast of Cuba. After repeated attacks by pirates, they moved the city inland and resettled in 1528. After Cuban independence from Spain in 1902, they changed the name to the Indian name "Camaguey."

The city rewards visitors with its colonial architecture, historic cathedrals, stone-paved streets, quiet *playas* (beaches), and graceful town squares. It became known as the "City of Churches" and was settled mostly by Catholics. Another aspect of Camaguey's uniqueness was the large earthenware clay pots, called "*Tinajones*." Residents used them for storing rainwater to drink. They are used today as garden monuments, or for practical use.

Camaguey became an important trading and industrial center, especially for the cattle and sugar businesses. Sugarcane fields brought jobs and economic stability. The city also became a crossroads for rail travel and was home to an international airport.

The city of Camaguey was a closed society and conservative in its way. People lived in the same houses and socialized with the same people all their lives.

More than anything, Camaguey was a place known for its love of art and culture. It was the birthplace of *Ignacio Agramonte,* an essential figure of the Ten Years War against Spain.

Camaguey was a beautiful city with plenty of charm. I would have spent most of my life enjoying its beauty if our lives had not been interrupted by Fidel Castro's Revolution.

VACATIONING IN PARADISE

Chapter 6

My parents and I in Varadero beach

After a time, my father's hard work paid off, giving us the luxury of traveling to the beach often. One beautiful weekend, my parents and I took our usual vacation in *Varadero Beach*. We always stayed at the *Vista Alegre Hotel*. This grand hotel had a wide porch overlooking the water. It had about twenty rooms with an open, elegant marquee.

The welcoming wooden Adirondack recliner chairs made it easy for us to enjoy the beach view and feel the island's breeze. All I could hear at night was the peaceful sounds of the crashing waves, which always helped me fall asleep.

As soon as I reached the beach, my heart leaped with joy. I stood there on the crisp white sand watching the locals sell a fruit called *Mamoncillos*. My parents cautiously watched me tear the end of the rind, as I squeezed the pinkish juice off the flesh into my mouth until there was nothing left. My parents always cautioned me as I ate them, "Helenita, be careful not to choke on the large seed!" Oh, how I loved to eat them.

With my bucket and pail at hand, I was ready to play. The sand was scorching, and it looked golden with tiny white specks. It sparkled like faraway stars taking in the sun.

Children were laughing and playing, and others were relaxing on the beach while enjoying the bright rays of sunlight. I still remember the smell from the ocean mixed with the sand. It brought me so much peace as if I were the only one there.

Every morning, my parents and I would walk to the beach. We would spend hours enjoying the tranquil blue waters of our paradise island. My father would throw me up in the air and catch me before I hit the water. My mother watched with apprehension, even though she knew my father would never drop me.

While visiting the beach, I remember meeting a little boy about my age. His name was Ricardito, which means little Richard. I thought he was the cutest boy I had ever met.

Ricardito didn't look like most of the Cuban boys I had met before, with their tanned skin, black hair, and dark eyes. No, he was different.

His skin was pale white. He had the most beautiful blue eyes I had ever seen. While our parents took a few pictures of us in a park nearby, Ricardito mostly ignored me.

I had many memories in Varadero beach, but also on another beach named Tarafa. There, my second cousin Erne wed a young man from America, with pale skin and green eyes. It was a beautiful tropical wedding.

I remember thinking to myself, *when I grow up, I will marry an American man, with pale skin and green eyes!* Soon after my cousin married, they left the island and migrated to New York. I never saw them again. These vacations didn't last very long, but the memories of our time together will always be there.

Our two-week vacation ended. It was time to travel back to our beautiful, humble home in Camaguey. All I could think about was seeing my nanny, *Elsa.* My nanny was chubby and blacker than anyone I had ever seen before.

Elsa was a hard-working woman, kind and compassionate. She not only took care of me, but she also cooked and cleaned as needed. Elsa was a single parent with six children, and I never heard her complain. She lived in an impoverished village where I remember her taking me with her to meet her family. My parents paid her well and always helped her with whatever her needs were.

Sometimes my parents would go for a ride in the evening and would take my nanny and me along with them. On the way back home, we would always play a game she made up called, find the nanny.

With her mouth closed, she would move around in the

FAMILY FUN AT THE BEACH

dark and pretended I couldn't find her. Then, she would start laughing, and suddenly, her shiny white teeth would glow in the dark. It tickled us so much that we would laugh hysterically until my parents finally hushed us up.

We finally arrived home, and my nanny gave me lots of hugs. I was very fortunate that she would stay the night with us whenever she was able to get her extended family to take care of her children. She practically lived with us. My father had built a small room for Elsa inside our home. Elsa wasn't just my nanny, she was part of our family and a great helper to my mother, who could not exert herself due to her heart condition.

I would have never imagined that one day soon, the relationship I had with my dear nanny would be a thing of the past.

A GLIMPSE OF FAMILY CHAOS!

Chapter 7

In the late 1950s, strange things happened in our family. Though I didn't have a clue what they all meant, I was old enough to sense that something was not right. I observed and questioned situations in my life and the lives of my parents that didn't quite add up. One of the first things I started noticing was that father didn't always come home for dinner. In fact, sometimes he wouldn't come home for days.

I remember one memorable birthday. My mother was preparing for my celebration. Mother dressed me up in one of my finest skirt and blouse ensembles. I must have had five or six petticoats on—the ones that itched your legs like crazy, no matter which way I moved. Since I had one hip slightly higher than the other, making my store-bought clothes look funny, my mother had most of my clothes made by a seamstress. Some of my dresses were made by my godmother, Maria Sabates, who was an exceptional seamstress.

I remember looking like a helium balloon, about to take flight in that skirt. My nails were sparkling clean, and my mother had pulled my hair back in such a tight ponytail that it looked as if I just had a facelift.

My mother had invited one of her brothers, Uncle Ñico, to my birthday party. Early that morning, he had come to help my mother decorate since my father was nowhere to be found. Both my parents enjoyed music, so she played her favorite Bolero songs. This slow romantic ballad originated on the island. Some of her selections for this special occasion were "Beny More, Celia Cruz, Olga Guillot," and many more. We had balloons, cake, and decorations all around the house. We were ready to start our party.

Uncle Ñico was a lot of fun to be around but was known for being dangerous at times. He would often bring his throwing knives over to our house, which he had mastered after much practice. Though he was skilled at it, I didn't find it the least amusing, especially when he would attempt to throw them at my mother, missing her by inches. This day was no exception. Ñico was standing near our compact kitchen between the dining room and the living room, where mother was. She told her brother that she wasn't in the mood to play.

"Ñico, don't start throwing those knives," she said.

My uncle just laughed. He looked at her from a distance of about ten feet and told her to be still––he was ready to launch his first knife.

I peeked from behind my bedroom door, petrified with fear. I thought my uncle was going to stab my mother for sure.

My mother was no fool. She knew that whether she liked it or not, Ñico would throw the knife at her. She stood as still as a statue. Before she could say anything, one of Ñico's knives came flying towards her, missing her head by mere centimeters. She was furious!

Furious, because he scared her half to death—furious because she hadn't heard from my father in several days—just plain mad!

Just as mother was going after my uncle to give him a piece of her mind, two people walked in the front door. One of them was my father, and the other one was Antonio Milla, his associate from work and a friend of the family. Milla and his wife, Flor, had been close friends of my parents for many years. More than once, Milla came to dad's rescue. Their entrance saved Ñico, but dad was in a heap of trouble.

My mother's face turned red. It almost looked like fire was coming out from her beautiful green eyes. My uncle decided to leave quickly to the patio, away from the war zone that was about to erupt.

As dad walked into the house, smiling as usual, but paler than a corpse, mother grabbed a butcher knife. She ran toward him—ready to do bodily harm. I believe she intended to incapacitate him for life.

"Don't hurt him! Don't hurt him!" I screamed.

My dad grabbed a dining room chair to protect himself, as though a ferocious lion was coming at him.

I heard my father scream out her name, "Sarah, Sarah! Stop, I can explain."

Milla, who was a strong man, disarmed my mother and calmed things down.

This wasn't the first time my father had seen my mother's wrath, but never with a deadly weapon. If I hadn't been so scared, it might have looked like a scene from a comedy in an old movie.

That day, mother had about enough of my father's nonsense, and she threatened to divorce him, which she had done many times before. However, somehow my father always persuaded her to stay.

My mom & dad standing on the steps of a Hotel in Varadero Beach.

My parents were romantics. When they were together, you could see how much they loved each other. However, from time to time, the same passion that drew them together also drove them apart.

Sometimes, dad would tell me that my mother was the only woman he had ever loved. Even though he had a funny way of showing it, I believed him.

Once the fighting stopped, they would make up and continue their love for one another. This kind of love kept them together each time the storms of life tossed them around.

After the crazy ordeal with my parents, my birthday party went on as planned.

MY MOTHER, ANTONIO MILLA & HIS WIFE FLOR IN A MIAMI BEACH HOTEL 1950'S.

EXCITEMENT ON NEW YEARS DAY

Chapter 8

Early in the morning on New Year's Day in 1959, an unexpected event took place on our beautiful island. My mother had just closed the windows of our dining room to block some air. Unseasonably cool air draped the island. Otherwise, a typical day. Nothing to warn us of the life-changing event about to occur. One that would signal the beginning of the worst days of our lives.

Elsa, my nanny, had fixed our breakfast this morning as usual. As we sat at our dining table, my mother served me one of our customary meals—toasted Cuban bread, cafe con leche (warm milk with a little bit of Cuban coffee), and ham croquettes, one of my favorite dishes. After I finished, I went to my room to take a short nap while my parents retired to the living room.

During my peaceful nap, I woke up to a loud noise coming from our living room. My parents had been listening to a radio program which they usually did after a filling meal. Suddenly, a loud voice interrupted the program.

"Batista has fled, Batista has fled! He has fled the island, and the rebels have won!"

Outside of our home, we heard what sounded like an enormous party going on. People were shouting, "Batista has fled, Batista has fled!"

I remember later that day my father took me to a nearby park to celebrate Batista's desertion of our country. People hugged. Some sang. Others gave speeches of triumph. I saw the presence of tanks and rebels in their green uniforms carrying machine guns on their shoulders.

One rebel we met handed me what seemed like an empty shell from one of their weapons. Maybe it was a real bullet. I couldn't tell the difference. Everyone looked ebullient.

The people cheered as the rebels marched in victory through the streets of Camaguey.

For some time, my parents had known that our country was in disarray during Batista's presidential term. For this reason, they wanted to believe that there was hope in the eyes of the *barbudos* (the bearded ones), as they were called. Unfortunately, nothing could have prepared us for the torrential storm of events that were about to erupt in our cities.

THE RALLY

Chapter 9

ME IN FRONT OF MY HOUSE IN CUBA

It was October of 1959, and I was now five years old. The weather was still humid, but the tropical breeze made the heavy air bearable. On this particular day, my dad had asked me if I wanted to go out with him to a special place. I immediately said, "Yes."

Despite my curiosity, I kept questions about our destination to myself.

My father was an industrious and social person. Occasionally, he would try to spend one-on-one time with me. It was not like he would take me to the park or fishing, no, he always preferred to take me to unusual places. That day began as any other special day for me, for no other reason than spending time with him.

As we left our house, he broke his silence and told me he was taking me to a political rally. I had no clue what he was talking about, but it didn't matter, I was still excited.

The rally was at a Plaza in our hometown of Camaguey. The leader who was speaking was the charismatic Fidel Castro.

Before approaching the front of the stage, where Castro stood to give his speech, my father said to me, "Helenita, let's hurry and find a place as close as we can, so I can find out who Fidel Castro really is."

I always found it funny when my father would kneel to my level and speak to me as if I was an adult. As a child, he always made me feel as if I was important enough to share his sentiments with me.

He grabbed my hand and pulled me toward the front of the crowd. His goal was to get a good look at this leader. He wanted to hear what Castro's plans were concerning the freedom of our country.

The crowd stood elbow-to-elbow. Standing room only. Father wanted to be in the front row so he could hear every word Castro said. I felt anxious and cramped. Unable to move.

This was the first time I had laid eyes on Castro. I can still picture him as he delivered a speech to the people. For a moment, I felt like he was scolding me. I wasn't sure what he was talking about, but I remember that he kept waving his pointer finger at the crowd as if to convince the people his promises were real. As far as I was concerned, they were.

My father had not been a fan of Batista, who had been the President of Cuba for a while. He said that Batista was full of corruption, and that change needed to happen on our island.

Though my father had no clue where Fidel Castro's power would take our country, he wanted to believe that Castro would bring change to the already discontented Cuban people, who by now were fed up with Batista's unfairness. However, he wasn't convinced that Castro was the answer to our country's problems.

As the rally was ending, I heard the people shouting, "Viva La Revoluciòn!" (Long live the revolution!)

My father pulled me out of the crowd, holding my hand in a tight grip. He practically dragged me all the way home. What I thought would be a fun day, turned out to be a stressful one, even for someone my age.

When we got home, dad told mom in an urgent voice, "Sarah, you would not believe what I heard! Castro's speech was so convincing. It was like he was offering the people, not only of Camaguey but our entire country, hope for a better future! It was all so believable, but something didn't seem right. There were too many promises. I don't believe he will be able to deliver them all!"

Even at my age, I could sense by my father's tone of

voice that something was terribly wrong. He had always been a man of discipline and seemed to have it together most of the time. But on this day, I saw him come unglued.

It was not long after the rally that my parents heard rumors of our leaders' past and present intentions. Many rebel groups were behind Castro, which culminated in the organization of criminal gangs. They committed every kind of misdeed while they were in the mountainous region of the Sierra Maestra, in the Province of Oriente, Cuba.

CAMILO CIENFUEGOS'S LAST INTERVIEW BY THE PRESS

MODERATOR, MY FATHER ARNALDO CEBRIAN DE QUESADA

Chapter 10

My father (Center) moderated an interview of Camilo Cienfuegos (Left) and Jorge Enrique Mendoza Reboredo

Camilo Cienfuegos was one of Fidel Castro's comrades. He was involved in the overthrow of Fulgencio Batista during the revolution in early 1959. Later Cienfuegos would serve in the Cuban Army's high command, fight the anti-Castro uprising, and play a role in implementing the regime's agrarian reform. He became a vital figure of the Cuban revolution.

Days passed after my father and I had attended the rally where Castro gave his speech. My life went on as usual. One early evening my mother and I had gotten home from a full day of running errands. Soon it would be dark, and my mother had permitted me to go out to our garden to chase the *Cocuyos* (fireflies). They would come out at night with bright flashing green lights when I least expected it. They fascinated me.

When I came inside to prepare for bed, I noticed that my mother was more anxious than usual. I figured that it was because my father might have been roaming around town without her, but I wasn't sure what it was.

On October 21, 1959, Fidel sent Camilo Cienfuegos to arrest another of Fidel's comrades, *Huber Matos.*

Huber Matos had also assisted Fidel Castro at the start of the revolution. He was also a supporter of the 26th of July Movement, which commemorated the attack in Santiago de Cuba's army barracks in 1953. Huber Matos became a high-ranking military commander of the Army in the Province of Camaguey.

Not too long after Matos' revolutionary triumph with Castro, he and some of his soldiers suspected that the revolution had been shifting toward a Communistic regime. He realized that he could no longer trust the government to accomplish a democratic system in Cuba.

In September, Matos had sent Castro a letter, resigning his position, which was not accepted. On October 19, 1959, Matos sent Castro a second letter of resignation. Fidel Castro, distraught with Matos, branded him as a traitor of the revolution. He had heard rumors that Matos was planning a counter-revolutionary uprising. A few days later, Camilo Cienfuegos arrested Huber Matos and his military adjutants.

Huber Matos was tried and sentenced to twenty years in a Cuban prison. Castro tried him for treason, despite there being no evidence of any conspiracy against the revolution.

It was October 23, 1959. My father had been working late at the radio station. It was around 8:00 at night, and he was supposed to be home no later than 7:00 that evening. He was running late. When he finally got home, I ran to him and embraced him.

He put me to bed and left my room. As I tried to fall asleep, I couldn't help but overhear my father telling my mother what happened at his workplace and the reason he was late.

Two of his associates called him at the radio station, asking him to act as a moderator at a television station, but they didn't tell him who would serve in the panel. Since my father's contribution as a moderator had always been voluntary, he told his co-workers that he couldn't do it because he was late getting home. However, just before he walked out the door, the phone rang again, so he decided to pick it up, in case it was something important. This time it was his boss, Don Pancho.

In an urgent tone, Don Pancho said to my father, "Drop everything you are doing! Report immediately to Channel

11 TV station. We have an urgent matter in our hands!"

After my dad got to the TV station, his boss finally told him what role he would play in the interview.

On October 23, 1959, my father Arnaldo Cebrian de Quesada acted as the moderator for Camilo Cienfuegos.

As my father explained the order of the interview, he turned it over to the panelist to question Camilo. The panel consisted of journalists Frank Prendes, Juan Abel Adan (Juvenil), and Manolo de la Torre. They asked about Matos' arrest and whether there had been a shift within the revolution toward a communist regime. For a while, the interview went on with many more pertinent questions that were asked by the panel, leaving my father with a lot more questions concerning our country's future.

Several days after the interview, Camilo Cienfuegos, Felix Rodriguez, and Luciano Fariñas Rodriguez, an experienced pilot, boarded a *Cessna 310* to travel from Camaguey to Havana. The plane disappeared during the night flight without a trace. Their disappearance remains a mystery.

Camilo and his men's' disappearance was the pivotal moment when my father realized that we were living in perilous times. In my father's published book, *Papa Pio,* he describes in further detail the conversation between the panel, the press, and my father's questions to Camilo. He wrote many pieces of literature and articles and appeared in video interviews concerning the televised program of that day. But that is his story, better told by him in his book.

MY FATHER AND HIS WORK ASSOCIATE, ANTONIO MILLA

RELIGIOUS AND PRIVATE SCHOOLS INDEFINITELY CLOSED

Chapter 11

When Batista fled the country, it left an open invitation for Fidel Castro to present himself as the savior of the Cuban people, which was an immense step in his crusade to gain control of Cuba.

Over several years, Castro grew his forces and continued attacks on the island, in which he gained many volunteers. Using guerilla warfare tactics, Castro and his men attacked Batista's forces, overtaking town after town. Batista's army weakened and collapsed.

After finishing my kindergarten year at Obrea elementary, I started first grade at *El Colegio Teresiano* (Teresiano Catholic school) in a nearby neighborhood. I was shy and withdrawn at home most of the time, but when I was at school, I felt free and uninhibited. I always found school as a getaway, not only to learn but also to laugh and play.

One of my fondest memories of going to school was

coming home at lunchtime for a few hours. My father would go back home for lunch at about the same time as I did.

My teacher at the Obrea School giving me a diploma.

Elsa, my nanny, made us lunch. After Dad and I would finish, we would take a *siesta,* a quick nap, together. I would tightly grip his camiseta or muscle T-shirt.

He would often wake up before I did, and he would have to pry my little fingers off his camiseta, without interrupting my peaceful sleep.

I never wanted to let him go. My father was my security and the one person that made me feel safe. I could have never imagined life without him.

There were other memories, like the day our school took us out on a field trip to a poverty-stricken village in the countryside. We were to deliver food to the poor.

Being in the Catholic faith taught me a lot about having compassion for people. Their love of giving never ceased.

When we arrived at the village, one of the nuns, Sister Caridad, handed me a grocery bag full of vegetables, fruits, and other items. She told me they had assigned me to a little girl about four years old. I was to wait for her to approach me before handing her the bag.

As I stood there on this dirt road, I saw a girl who

I LOVED BEING IN THE MARCHING BAND IN SCHOOL.

looked hauntingly sad. She had a torn white dress, almost paper-thin from wear and tear. Her feet were filthy from walking on the dirt roads barefoot.

She had almond-shaped, dark brown eyes and beautiful long eyelashes. Her expression told a story of sadness, hunger, and abandonment. For all I knew she had no one to love her and no safe place to sleep.

As she came closer to me, I could tell she was scared. When I handed her the bag full of food, she grabbed it and ran off quickly. I watched her run until she faded from my view. I walked back to the school bus, thinking of what I had just witnessed.

Something inside of me almost felt as if that little girl was me, that somehow, I could have been born into poverty. Did I imagine this? I said to myself. As far as I knew, that was not the case—I was a privileged child. Life had treated me well up to that point, even with all the chaos happening in our country, I still felt blessed.

In the weeks following our field trip, I noticed a lot of tension and whispering in our school, though I didn't quite understand the complexity of it all. As I continued to attend classes, I noticed that some of my classmates were no longer sitting at their desks. They seemed to have vanished without a trace.

Even more disturbing was when I noticed that some of the nuns were also disappearing. I did not understand why, but it all would be revealed to me soon.

One morning after being in class for several hours, my parents came into my classroom. I thought it strange when they approached my teacher, Sister Edna. For a moment, it scared me because I thought I was in trouble. When she called me up front, I would have never expected what happened next.

As I joined my parents and Sister Edna, I noticed the seriousness on their faces. As my parents and I walked out the door, no one spoke a word. We walked in complete silence. We got into our car and drove away.

A few days later, my parents and I were driving around town, when I realized that we were slowly driving past my school. As I looked out the car window, I got excited, thinking I was going back, but my excitement was interrupted by what I saw.

The Government had boarded the double oversized wooden doors to my school. As we drove by, I wondered if I would ever return to school and see my classmates and teachers again.

Me waiting for the bus.

Looking back at my childhood, I will never forget a particular day when I took part in a marching band parade. Though I do not remember the occasion, I vividly remember wearing a white marching band uniform with a hat like a Shako band hat. I still recall how happy I was when they chose me for this special occasion. These festivities and many more will always remain in my memory.

At this point, Castro had nationalized both religious and private schools, which were later closed indefinitely. The Government had seized them and eventually turned them into government or technical schools. They implemented Educational Reform Law, which declared that education was now the responsibility of the revolutionary Government, imposing its Communist ideology on children. Schools became the regime's indoctrination centers.

I had hopes that one day I would return to my school. I often asked my mother, "Why am I not in school, Mami?"

I never received an answer.

RELIGIOUS PERSECUTIONS

Chapter 12

My first Communion. I am 4th row back, 2nd from left.

Many rebel soldiers roamed the streets of Camaguey after Fidel Castro, and his men took over our country. Some rebels were young. They believed that Cuba could become a better place under the leadership of Castro. However, these callow men lacked the scope and understanding to see the truth. These idealists set themselves up for the lies Castro's government was feeding them.

Castro's speeches became stronger as he gained favor with the Cuban people. Although some were aware of Castro's involvement with student activist groups, knowing the danger this represented, most people were blind regarding his rancor toward authority.

Heading to church amid religious tension.

As the years went by, the relationship between Cuba and the United States became strained. Castro, who had assured the world when he took over Cuba that he was not a Communist, soon enough turned out to be precisely that.

Toward the end of 1961, Castro announced in a televised speech the socialist nature of his regime. Fidel Castro finally admitted to the Cuban population that he was a Marxist-Leninist and that he would be one until the end of his life. He announced that Communism would be the dominant force in Cuban politics.

The Cuban people had wanted Batista gone and democracy restored, but instead of restoration, Castro took the country and its people in the opposite direction. He consolidated his power into a communist dictatorship and sought the support of the Soviet Union.

My parents didn't always see eye to eye in attending church. My father believed that believing in God was enough for him, though he had great faith in God. My mother, who was a devout Catholic, prayed regularly and went to church faithfully.

It was a Sunday morning, and my parents and I went to mass in one of the many churches in the center of Camaguey Province.

On this day, my father went to church with us with no fuss.

I remember walking into our beautiful church. It was fuller than usual. We found three empty seats near the back of the church, close to the massive wooden double doors.

The priest began his ritual prayers. The congregation repeated after him. I believe some of it was in Latin and some in Spanish. I pretended to follow along with everyone else. Though I couldn't make out a word they were saying, I silently moved my lips.

After about thirty minutes, my father got up, leaned toward my mother, whispered something in her ear, then walked out of the church. I wanted to go with him, but my mother held on to my hand.

Halfway through mass, as the adults bowed in prayer, I heard the wooden doors open and slammed violently shut. I turned around to see what was happening.

I saw *los milicianos* (the rebels) dressed in their olive-green uniforms with caps on their heads. Mother pulled me close to her.

Many of the rebels wore rosaries with large crosses around their necks. My father often said that the insurgents had blinded the Cuban people with their holy appearance. Some people thought of Fidel as a saint who had come to rescue our people from Batista's rule.

With machine guns propped on their shoulders, they

marched through the aisles of the church as though they were on a mission.

They smelled sweaty as they marched by my aisle. Boots clomped towards the front of the church. They didn't look to the right or left; they seemed focused on silencing the priest and the congregation.

I could hear the people praying louder. It was almost deafening. With so many people in front of me, I could hardly see what was happening at the altar, but I wiggled myself a little into the aisle while struggling to loosen my mother's grip on me.

I vaguely remember what was truly going on in front of the church, though to my recollection, it was a very unpleasant sight.

The louder the rebel got, the louder the congregation prayed. I was confused about what was going on, but I remained calm.

I glanced up at my mother to see if she would tell me that everything would be alright, but I heard nothing from her. I bowed my head and prayed. It was a simple, brief prayer, I said, "God protect us!"

Right after I said "Amen", my mother pulled me from the pew and ran towards the exit door. Something terrible was about to happen. I could feel it.

With my mother dragging me behind her, I felt the urge to look back. As we were stepping out the doors, I heard the first shot inside the church. People screamed. Others ran in a panic, trying to escape the horrific chaos that these rebels had unleashed on us. It all seemed to have happened in slow motion.

I was confused and horrified, but we got out of the church unharmed. When we made it home, mother was beside herself. The trauma we had just experienced left both of us shaking.

When my father arrived home that night, I couldn't help but hear my parents talking about the grim events happening all over our country.

That was our home church. I had been baptized and done my first communion there. My parents and godparents, Jose and Maria Sabates, were present. It was a place where our family took part in processions and religious parades.

As you can see, this is where we shared our lives with friends and family. Now, instead of a place of worship, it had become a cauldron of violence.

For several weeks after our experience with the shooting during Mass, my parents decided not to return to our church.

Although my parents were now more cautious of our whereabouts, they didn't want to give in to the fear that had been introduced into our lives. One day mother and I decided to attend one of our many religious processions in the center of Camaguey.

My Aunt Emma, and my two cousins, Emmita and Mirtha, were already at the procession when my mother and I got to the square where the church of *La Caridad*, was located. There were rebel soldiers everywhere. With no warning, shooting broke out in the center of the square. At first, I thought they were firecrackers like the ones I had heard when attending carnivals in the streets of Camaguey during special festivities.

Unfortunately, the sounds were not of a celebration; instead, they were the deafening sounds of gunfire and people screaming as they ran for their lives. As we all ran for safety, my hand slipped from my mother's grip. She screamed, "Run, Helenita, run!"

I was seven years old, and for the first time in my life, I felt genuine fear. Scared, and in a panic, I kept running and calling my mother, "Mami, Mami, where are you?"

I'd lost her.

I was bewildered amid so many people running for safety; the gunfire kept getting louder and louder. I was so scared and lost that I froze and stopped running. As I stood there crying in the middle of all these panicking strangers, I suddenly felt a hand on my shoulder.

It was my oldest cousin, Emmita, who had not taken her eyes off me since I was the youngest of the three of us.

She grabbed me and my other cousin, Mirtha, and started running fearfully fast, hoping a stray bullet would not hit us. As we ran, the gunfire never ceased. Thank God, we reached Marina's house safely.

Marina was one of my mother's aunts, who lived near one corner of the plaza. My cousins and I waited until my mother and my Aunt Emma made their way to where we were. After a while, my father came and picked us up.

After we got home that night, I heard my father tell my mother, "Our new leader has kept one of his most dramatic reform secrets from us. Now that he has declared himself a Communist, the major thrust of his crime is against all religions."

Castro had convinced these sincere priests that he espoused the same beliefs as them. However, by now, the Cuban institutions, especially the religious organizations, realized the cost of their decision to elect Fidel Castro. He directed the major assault of the communist regime against all religions, whether Catholic or Christians of various denominations or anyone who did not submit to the proclaimed revolution. They arrested many men of the cloth for suspicion of not embracing the Communist ideology.

COMMUNIST CONTROL

Chapter 13

From left to right: My mom, my cousins Emmita and Mirtha, my aunt Emma, and my great aunt Marina.

As a young child, I couldn't understand why there was so much anger and division in our cities. I began hearing shouts of *"Paredon!"* (The wall, where executions took place). There were televised executions in our cities without any regard for protecting our young, innocent eyes and ears. For this reason, my father felt the need to give me a crash course in our country's history. He knew that the things my young eyes were witnessing would affect me for the rest of my life. He wanted to make sure that I understood the price a country would pay when adopting a *Socialist, Communist country.*

Though I had always felt safe in my home, in my church, and my city, things began to change radically. I no longer felt safe anywhere.

As the days went by, there seemed to be no order in our city. Terrorist acts happened regularly in our country. They would bomb buildings and sabotage industries and commercial properties, especially those owned by *American* companies.

My uncle, Dario, who owned a business for a long time, had to work for the government for a year, after his uncle, who was also his business partner, left the country to live in Spain. At the end of that year, he had to surrender his business with all its content. However, that was not the only thing he had to surrender to the authorities.

One late night and without knocking, several rebel soldiers entered Dario's home. He and his family were all inside. The rebels searched the house as if they owned it. Two of the machine gun-toting rebels entered my cousins, Emmita, and Mirtha's room. Since my cousins did not know the rebels' intentions, they didn't say a word. Frightened, they wrapped their arms tightly around each other.

The rebels kept asking them for their father's electric razor, but the girls were too scared to answer them. Even though there was no logic or reasoning for what the rebels were asking, they seemed to take pleasure in taunting and humiliating them. At that moment, my Aunt Emma came into their room and told them that my uncle didn't own an electric razor.

After a few minutes of the rebels searching my aunt and uncle's home, they started shouting at them, "All of you have to get out now, this house belongs to the revolution!" My uncle, frightened for his family's safety, gathered them together, grabbing a few things to take with them. Exasperated that my uncle and his family were not moving fast enough, the rebels kept yelling at them. When my uncle attempted to leave with his family through the front door, he quickly realized that the rebels had sealed it shut.

One of the rebels began to yell again, "Everyone out of the house, you no longer own this property! All of you must exit through the garage immediately!"

With sadness and anger that my uncle couldn't even express for fear of being arrested, Dario, my Aunt Emma and my two cousins, Emmita and Mirtha, walked out of their home, leaving everything behind, never to return.

That night my uncle and his family went to stay with Marina at her house. In the morning they took a taxi to Havana. They spent two days in a hotel until they received their legal papers. Once they did, they headed to the airport.

When they arrived at the Havana airport, the rebels searched them along with the others waiting to leave for the United States. They asked my uncle what he did for a living as if they didn't know. He answered and said that he had owned a business. He told them he had a letter from the Cuban government saying that he had surrendered everything to the proper officials and had permission to leave the country.

In the interrogation room, they told my uncle that he had to return to Camaguey and get a seal of approval from the department of labor to legalize it. They said that he was not allowed to leave the country on that day, but that his wife and his two daughters could board the plane.

On March 31, 1962, my Aunt Emma and my two cousins got on the plane alone. However, my uncle had to stay behind.

The change and sadness that leaving our country brought to our families is indescribable. My oldest cousin, Emmita, didn't speak a word when she arrived in the United States until she reunited with her father.

Fortunately for my uncle, Marina and the taxi driver had not left the airport yet, and my uncle traveled almost 200 miles back to Camaguey to get the seal.

After my uncle had gotten the required documents he needed, he went back to the Havana airport once again. They sat him at the *G2* (the interrogation office), asking him more impertinent questions and trying to find something else they could use to keep him from leaving the country. Then, as though by divine intervention, they called his name to board the plane.

A previous passenger, who had not been able to board the plane, gave my uncle the seat. On April 3, 1962, they allowed my Uncle Dario to leave Cuba. On this day, he joined his family in the United States to live a life of freedom.

I have so many fond memories with my cousins at their house in Cuba. We used to play in the backyard whenever I came to spend the day with them. My youngest cousin,

Mirtha, used to sling her baby dolls up on the rooftop of their house, and for some reason, I always laughed at her mischievous actions

Many children and adults who had no choice but to leave our country and embrace the unknown in a foreign land experienced immense trauma throughout their lifetime.

My other uncle, Dagoberto, on my father's side, who had been very successful in the candy-making business, also had to surrender his manufacturing company to the government.

He had worked so hard and gone through so many struggles to build his own business from the ground up, that to have it taken away was pure evil.

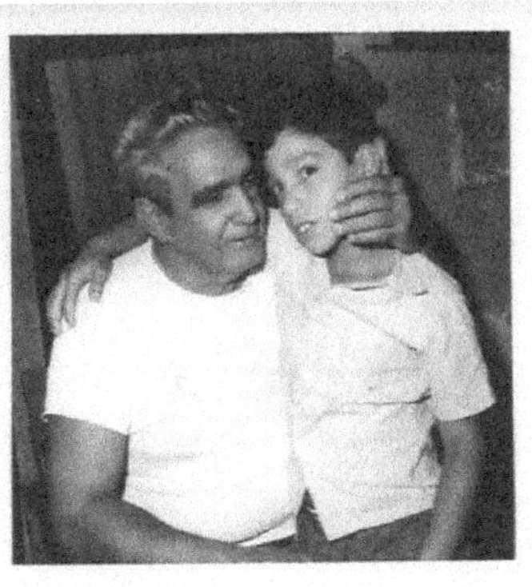
MY UNCLE DAGOBERTO AND HIS SON

I remember him taking me to his candy manufacturing company and giving me all the candy my little heart desired. I can still see myself as a child, unwrapping the little red candy and savoring its sweet cherry flavor in my mouth. My uncle Dagoberto was never able to leave Cuba and I never saw him again. The Communist government ripped away everything we loved and cherished. However, the one thing they could not take from us was our memories.

The repression showed its strength. Executions of anyone suspected of being anti-Communists increased. Whispers of awful stories about the atrocities against those who did not embrace Castro's ideology traveled about the country.

Forced labor, deportation, beatings, and executions were an almost everyday occurrence. There were also rumors of various plots to overthrow Castro by the Americans whom they called "The Imperialistic Yankees."

My second cousin, Luisito, on my father's side, was taken to El Paredon. Luisito was a strong man full of convictions for the Cuba he loved. He was not easily intimidated, and he told my dad he wasn't afraid to die for his country.

Luisito's last words before they shot him were, "Cowards, you may destroy my body, but you will never destroy my soul!"

The leader of the death squad shouted, *"Preparen! Apunten! Fuego!"* (Ready, Aim, Fire!)

First, the rebels tortured Luisito, shooting him in several parts of his body while humiliating him and yelling, "Die like gusanos! (a worm!)"

My father was a witness to this horrific crime. He said that the rebels let Luisito suffer from the wounds on his body before finishing him with a bullet to the head, execution-style.

These were some of the injustices that many innocent lives suffered for speaking out against an oppressive government.

There was much bloodshed at El Paredon. The executions began with the killings of Batista's men and continued toward those who did not adhere to the communist beliefs. These executions were not only at El Paredon.

They were throughout the island. Many were also in the Sierra Maestra, where Fidel Castro, his brother Raul, Che Guevara and other rebels committed all types of crimes.

Luisito's only crime was speaking against the injustices the revolution had brought to the people of Cuba by Castro's regime.

They watched people closely. If the secret police were told by *los chivatos* (the snitches) that anyone was against the government, they didn't hesitate to take them into headquarters to interrogate them. There were no fair trials, either. If they couldn't find any reason other than opposition to their political views, they would make up a crime that would fit the punishment of their choice. Hatred was the new norm.

Jails were packed. No one trusted anyone anymore. Neighbors spied on neighbors, and the government expected the people to give up all allegiances for the good of the revolution.

Obligations to the family and loyalty to friends were no longer priorities in the eyes of Castro's twisted government. An island that was known for family closeness became a divided country.

My parents, my uncle Dario holding my cousin Emmita, and other family members during better times.

AMBUSH IN OUR BACKYARD

Chapter 14

One early morning, the deafening cluster sounds of machine-gun fire jolted me out of a deep sleep. Over the din, I heard my mother cry out, "Helenita, don't move! Don't move!"

What was happening? As I sat up, I had no idea what was going on, but after a few seconds, I recognized the *rat-a-tat, rat-a-tat* noise coming from outside my bedroom window.

Through the walls of my house, I heard my mother shouting, "Oh my God, oh my God, please help us!"

Despite the noise and commotion of the gunfire, all I could focus on was on my mother's continuous yelling.

"Don't get up from your bed, Helenita, stay still until we get you!"

I did what I was told. I laid back down and covered myself up to right below my eyes. My hands trembled as I grasped my blanket, waiting for my parents to come and save me.

The horror in my parents' voices was evident.

In my dimly lit room, I saw my parents crawling on the

granite floor toward me, as if they were soldiers in a war, avoiding being hit by bullets. More gunshots rang. My body froze, not yet registering what was happening. After a few more moments, I finally realized they were the same loud sound of the machine guns I had heard once before.

As the noise continued, I had that feeling of being trapped in a nightmare. When my parents got to me, my father whispered, "Helenita, be very quiet, the rebels are right outside your window!"

They pulled me under my bed. We huddled together, shaking and afraid.

We were there for what seemed like hours. Until suddenly, for a moment, the gunfire ceased. The calm before the storm.

Then we heard what was to be the last screams right outside our back door. "Let us in, please! Let us in! It's us! It's us!"

My father wanted to open the door and help them, thinking they were the anti-communist, but my mother, fearing a trap, said, "No, Arnaldo, we don't know who they are!"

Just as my mother had told my dad, "No!" the machine guns resumed firing. This time, screams accompanied the bullets.

Finally, silence fell. When my parents felt it was safe to come out, we crawled out from under my bed. They told me to stay in my bedroom, close to the floor in case the shooting started back up. My parents then went to see if anyone was still outside.

I was still frightened by what had transpired a few

ME SITTING IN FRONT OF THE BACKYARD WALL WHERE THE AMBUSH OCCURRED.

moments before, but my curiosity got the best of me. I cracked my bedroom door open and peeked outside where my parents were.

What I saw outside caused the acid in my stomach to churn. There was blood all over our flowerbeds my mother had once planted in our backyard.

There were rebels surrounding our home and they told my parents that there was a dead body on the other side of our concrete wall. We had no way of knowing if the dead body belonged to a rebel or the underground anti-communists who might have been banging on our back door for asylum.

For over a month, we constantly were hearing of gunshots and bombs throughout our island. Ever since Castro had aligned himself as a communist leader, there had been underground groups meeting to discuss how they could overthrow Castro's government. Now Castro's rebels were hunting them down, literally right in our backyard. Hundreds, and eventually thousands, of counterrevolutionaries were being lined up and shot against El Paredon, the same way they executed my second cousin, Luisito.

These events caused an emotional shock that eventually, I hid deep within my being. Disturbing images lingered in my head, leading me to accept my past by denying its existence.

It wasn't until I learned to confront the truth of my hidden memories that a breakthrough revealed the ugliness of what I had witnessed as a child.

LETTING GO

Chapter 15

EVERYTHING IN THIS PICTURE & OUR HOME HAD TO BE SURRENDERED TO THE AUTHORITIES

Eventually, things calmed down some—or so I thought. A few weeks later, I was in for another surprise. One morning, while I was entering my bedroom, I found my mother packing some of my clothes in a small suitcase. I asked her why she was packing my belongings, but her reply was vague.

She tried to reassure me that everything would be all right, but I didn't believe her. By her perplexed look, I don't think she did either. She got irritated with me and said not to ask her any more questions. She told me to sit in the living room with my father.

Before I left the bedroom, I asked her one more question, "Mami, why are you not packing my toys?"

Again, she said, "Please, do not ask me any more questions!"

Her reply annoyed me, but I obeyed her anyway and went to where my dad was sitting. As I walked into the living room, I noticed that there were two small suitcases next to his legs, which aroused my curiosity even more. He looked so sad. His head was bowed down. It almost looked like he had been praying. I was getting nervous and didn't understand why anything else in our home was not packed.

A few minutes later, I heard loud voices outside our porch. Six rebels burst through our front door, storming uninvited into our living room. I stood still for a moment and looked at my dad, not knowing what was about to happen.

MY MOTHER LOVED THIS MIRROR.

Before my father said anything, one rebel shouted at my dad, "You must leave now, this is property of the new proclaimed government!"

There they were, the same familiar men in olive green uniforms I had seen at the church, unshaven and with large sweat rings under their arms.

A burly government official yelled, "Hurry and leave the premises!"

I was getting accustomed to seeing the barbudos, or "the bearded ones." They seemed to be everywhere. I inched closer to my dad for fear that one of them would take me, but they went past me and walked around the inside of our home.

As my mother entered the living room, I asked her, "Where are we going, and where is my nanny?"

This time she didn't even look at me—that was my sign to hush! I noticed that my father and my mother exchanged glances, making the nonverbal agreement not to say anything that might jeopardize us.

The rebels looked around the house and smiled with pleasure at what they saw. My mother told me to pick up

IN FRONT OF OUR HOME WITH ONE OF THE DOLLS I HAD TO LEAVE BEHIND.

my suitcase. They reminded us that our house belonged to the Revolution.

We had to vacate the premises immediately. However, before we walked outside, one rebel stared at my mother up and down.

I could see my father's face turning red with anger, but he felt helpless. He feared that if he said anything, it might give these rebels a reason to take him for interrogation, leaving us alone with them. My mother just kept her eyes on my father and me, trying to stay focused.

As the three of us walked out of the home my father had built for us, we glanced at all the contents in our living room one last time. All that he had worked so hard to provide for our family was now gone. These rebels confiscated everything, including my toys along with the television my parents had bought in Miami, Florida when they had visited there. My parents traded all our worldly possessions so that one day we could be free.

There we were, walking together hand in hand, the three of us—my father leading my mother and me as we stared back at our home one more time. I believe we all had an eerie suspicion that we would never see our home again.

As we were walking toward our *1957 Chevrolet,* I thought we would get in our car and drive away as far as we could. However, as we passed by our car, I realized that the rebels had also taken possession of our vehicle.

A FRIEND AND I LEANING ON OUR LIGHT YELLOW 1957 CHEVROLET. THIS TOO THE GOVERNMENT CONFISCATED.

I knew the time had come to let go of everything we owned. We now had nothing but a few things my parents had packed in our three small suitcases and the clothes on our backs. The last thing I saw of our home was the iron cutout silhouette image of my father with his microphone on our front storm door, depicting his profession as a newscaster.

MY PARENTS SITTING ON OUR FRONT PORCH. THE DOOR WAS GLASS AND HAD A METAL CUT OUT OF A MAN'S FACE SPEAKING UNTO A MICROPHONE.

A NEW TENSION FILLED OUR HOME

Chapter 16

After they forced us out of our own home, we went to live at my Aunt Hilda's house. My mother reassured me it would only be for a little while. Hilda was one of my father's sisters. I loved going to her house and visiting with her and the little Papillon-looking dog they had. This little dog had long hair draped on his raised ears that made him look like a butterfly.

One early evening I heard my mother crying. My father was telling her, "Sarah, if they do not allow us to leave the country, we will find a boat or a raft to escape this communist government! I'm willing to take whatever risk for us to live in a free society. I would rather die at sea a free man than die in a country that will keep us in chains!"

As my father held my mother tight, he made her this promise, "I will make a plan, I will keep us safe!"

His words were powerful. However, he knew his plan would be a challenge if the government wouldn't let us leave.

"I'm in complete agreement, my love," she replied.

In the meantime, my father took every precaution not to get caught planning our escape. Our journey to get out of Cuba had begun.

As days passed by, the discussions concerning leaving Cuba became more frequent. My father was continually investigating how we could leave the island. All around us, terrible things were happening. By now, people were panicking, not knowing what would become of them if they didn't adhere to the communist regime. Those who were counterrevolutionaries were taking drastic measures to leave our country. Exiting the island was not guaranteed to anyone.

My father wanted to do everything as legally as possible, so he began the paperwork immediately. Since my father had resigned from his job, there was not much more we could offer the government in exchange for our freedom. For this reason, we had to petition the few people my parents could trust.

A new tension-filled our home. Chivatos (snitches) in our city had turned our names into the Communists headquarters, *El Gedo (G2).* They suspected that we were anticommunists and wanted to leave the country. My mother was worried for our safety. They considered us traitors against the revolution. We had now become known as gusanos (worms). The disturbing events happening in Cuba made it even more urgent that we leave the country as soon as possible.

In 1961, the *Bay of Pigs* happened. My parents and I had heard through word of mouth of this tragedy shortly afterward. It had also aired on the radio.

The number of Cuban exiles already in the United

States amounted to thousands. The Kennedy Administration took in the threat of Moscow's meddling in America via Cuba seriously.

The United States continued with the previous Eisenhower government, which was to continue the training of brigades by the Central Intelligence Agency to combat Communism. This invasion into Cuba was planned by Cuban exiles and supported by the United States government.

The plan was to land in a remote swampy area on the southern coast of Cuba. When the Cuban exiles, known as the *2506 Brigade,* landed at the Bay of Pigs, Castro had ordered his troops to confront the invaders on that swampy beach. After less than a day of fighting, there were hundreds killed, and some taken prisoners. For my parents, this was enough evidence to know that no change would come to our island any time soon.

FOOD SHORTAGE

Chapter 17

By now, my father hadn't been working for a while. They declared all our savings nonexistent. Money was tight, but being the resourceful man he was, he provided for us the bare necessities.

All newspapers, radio, and television were censored, monitored, and even silenced. My father could no longer express his freedom of speech. He resigned after being told that he could no longer give the news as he saw it. Tension in our cities exploded. The people that once trusted and respected my father's voice on the radio, now plotted to turn him into the authorities.

My Aunt Hilda's kitchen cabinets were nearly empty. The food shortage was now becoming a problem, and my parents struggled to keep food on our table. One day, I remember standing in an unending line with my mother. We waited for hours before reaching the doors to the grocery store to buy food. I was fidgety and tired of standing, but I could see the frustration in my mother's face.

After several hours of standing and waiting, we had only three people ahead of us. When the storekeeper came out, he announced, "Sorry, we're all out of meat! We are all out of everything. Come back tomorrow!"

My mother was furious. She ran all the way home, dragging me along. I could barely keep up. When we got back, my mother told my father what had happened. The government was preparing to establish a new system of rationing our food. Our new leader had proposed talk of a small ration book. The listings dictate how many grams of food each family could get. Parents were worried about how they would feed their children. The confusion baffled everyone.

My health had been poor for a while, and the shortage of nutrition was not making it any better. A few years before the food shortage I contracted the measles, developing chronic bronchitis, which had now turned into asthma, weakening my lungs further. Trips to the hospital for my respiratory treatments became frequent.

My parents were getting low on money, so they had to use home remedies and unconventional medicines to ease my constant coughs and labored breathing.

One of those unique rituals was *"Fire Coupling."* It went something like this: My father would wrap a cotton ball saturated with Vodka on the tip of a steel pair of scissors. He then would light it up with a match inside a glass cup. They would then place it on my stomach, and somehow it was supposed to cure all kinds of ailments. Who knew? Please don't try this at home! I have no clue if it worked or not. I still suffer from respiratory problems.

Contributing to the many other health issues I already had, I was also allergic to cows' milk. My parents would have to travel to a nearby farm. There they bought goat's milk for me to drink.

By now, everything was regulated by the government,

making things worse. Our trips to the farm were becoming more difficult every day. Because of the food shortage, I became anemic, and my health deteriorated rapidly. My parents were getting genuinely concerned.

Castro's speeches became stronger as he gained favor with the Cuban people. He spoke of free medical care, free education, even promises of modernizing farming practices so that everyone would have enough to eat. He spoke these things and more all over Cuba.

Castro told the people that wealth would no longer divide them. The government would offer equality for all people. My parents knew that this system of control would never work correctly. Castro failed to mention that they would lose their most valuable possession, their freedom.

UNDERGROUND SCHOOL

Chapter 18

It had been almost a year since I had been out of school. My parents had deliberately not enrolled me in the organized government school. They had realized that Castro's government was not in agreement with our beliefs concerning the new educational changes. My parents knew that if the wrong people found out about me not being in school, they would be in danger of being arrested or worse.

Rumors circulated that every child was going to be taught faithfulness to the Revolution, even above their parents. They had implemented a communist educational system, where all children would be sent to the fields to help with the sugarcane harvest. They would also make them go to reform schools to learn Marxism and Leninism, along with Communist ideology. All this talk frightened my parents. They didn't know what to do or who to believe, so they kept me hidden for as long as possible, but they were still concerned for my developmental education.

Education was crucial to my parents. They opted to take some risks in getting me educated. I was now almost eight years old. One morning before daybreak, my mother draped a sweater over my head. She put her arm around me and steered me rapidly down the sidewalk.

Even though it seemed rather strange to me, I decided not to ask questions. A few minutes later, we reached a set of descending stairs, which led to a small door. After knocking twice on the door, a woman named Cordelia greeted us. I immediately noticed she had several other children in her care.

This school was underground, both literally and figuratively. My mother left me there, and I spent many hours studying in the company of several other children. My parents had warned me that if anyone asked questions unless it was my teacher, I was to say I knew nothing.

Not long after I began attending this secret underground school, a frightening noise interrupted our peaceful little class. Several men in uniforms stormed into the room where we were. I tried to look calm, fearing that they would hurt us, but inside I was terrified.

My teacher and all of us children huddled together as one rebel yelled at us, "Move it!"

With his weapon in hand, he waved us towards the exit door. We all hurried and did what the rebels told us to do. They took the teacher and us children to the local communist headquarters. We were all interrogated. The rebels lured us children with candy so that we would give them information. A militia woman was sitting on a large chair, with one leg propped up on a stool. Her machine gun rested on one of her knees. She smiled at me and offered me more candy in exchange for information about my parent's whereabouts.

However, after I ate the candy she gave me, I said to her,

"I'm sorry, but I know nothing."

I didn't know much about communism, but I knew enough that what they wanted me to tell them was whether my parents were loyal to El Comandante, Fidel Castro.

Exposing our secrets could have cost us our lives. I was now beginning to realize that communism wasn't a good thing.

After interrogating our teacher, she had no other choice than to give the rebels information on how to contact our parents.

Eventually, the rebels contacted my parents to pick us up. When they arrived, they, too, were interrogated. Since the officials could not prove that my parents were against the government, we were able to leave. However, our teacher wasn't so lucky. After her interrogation, they put her in jail, and we never heard from her again.

By now, we knew that the government didn't need an excuse to put you behind bars. If they couldn't find you guilty of a crime, they would make up something and attach it to your file, accusing you of a crime that you had not committed.

I wasn't much of a talker as a young child, but with all the chaos happening in our city, I began to ask a lot of questions. One day I asked my father what would become of the other children that didn't attend an underground school.

My dad explained, "Some of those students will become the children of the new Revolution. They will become the militiamen and women of Cuba's future. They will become revolutionaries, Fidelistas (followers of Fidel) or informers and spies."

It concerned me that those children might not grow up in the safety of their parents. Instead, it sounded like they would be controlled by the government.

Anyone suspected of being anti-communist would face harsh consequences. They watched my parents closely after their interrogation at headquarters. This phase of my formal education was remarkably brief. This season in our lives marked the beginning of confiding in no one, of living a lie to protect our family.

CHRISTMAS MEMORIES IN CAMAGUEY

Chapter 19

Noche Buena (Christmas Eve) at the farm.

It was customary in our culture to celebrate Christmas. I only remember one Christmas with my parents in Cuba, but it was a memorable one. For me, it was always an exciting time watching mother preparing for the holidays. She had a knack for decorating, and this day was no exception.

Our Christmas tree was not the usual green tree with a lot of trimmings. Instead, my mother would have a branch-like tree cut and painted white. She then would hang brightly colored ornaments on each branch. She would also recreate a miniature village town with snow at the base of the tree, and our nativity scene was next to it. For me, it was always a magical day.

Christmas night was always fun for the entire family. Cuban Christmas is *Noche Buena*, which translates as "good night', but refers to Christmas eve. I remember going to Juanita's parent's farm on Christmas Eve. She was my parents' godchild. Juanita came from a very poor upbringing. They lived in a hut like home. Eventually, they had managed to buy the farm with hard work and determination. I remember us playing inside of a *palangana* full of water (a large metal basin.)

The farm was filled with all kinds of animals to delight a town-bred child like me—chickens, sheep, goats, horses, cats, and yes, scary dogs too. By sunset, they were finishing roasting their traditional hog, and then it was time to eat, with delicious lechon asado (roasted hog), white rice, black beans, fried plantains, yucca, and more.

Then there was dessert, turrones. These are a southern European nougat confection, typically made of honey, sugar, and egg white with toasted nuts, shaped in a rectangular tablet.

There were both hard and soft ones, but my favorites were the hard ones, with its wafer-like covering. Cuban people love to eat. You were guaranteed not to leave hungry.

There were campesinos (farmers) with their twelve-string Spanish guitars and a lot of dancing to go along with the music. We indeed had a wonderful time with friends

RIDING A HORSE AT LA FINCA

(THE FARM)

and family. There were spotlights strung above the tables. Everything was perfect for celebrating this splendid occasion. The sound of children playing around the adults was the icing on the cake.

Though Christmas was a favorite of mine, I have to say that January sixth was even better. On this day, we celebrated *Los Tres Reyes Magos* (The Three Wise Men), who had once visited the child, Jesus, with gifts of gold, frankincense, and myrrh. My parents told me that because of its symbolic nature, the wise men would also

bring me gifts every year on this special day. This day was something like celebrating Santa Claus in America.

On one particular January sixth, I'd woken up to find a big baby doll with its crib, along with many other dolls and toys under the tree.

However, these were not the only presents I received on that day. On our front porch, there was a beautiful wooden swing my father had custom-made, especially for me. To my surprise, it was full of more toys.

There was an Italian doll in a blue dress, one of my favorites. There was also a beautiful ballerina with movable arms and legs, and many other toys. My very favorite was a life-size *payaso* (clown) that was taller than me.

Even though the atmosphere in all of Cuba had been tense, Cuban families continued to celebrate our traditional holidays.

Eventually the Cuban government restricted all religious practices. We had no clue that these joyful moments of celebration with our families and friends would become a thing of the past.

CELEBRATING LOS TRES REYES MAGOS

SAYING MY GOODBYES

Chapter 20

PART OF MY FAMILY. SOME OF WHOM I NEVER SAW AGAIN.

Knowing that my parents were preparing our exit out of Cuba, saying goodbye to our friends and family would not be easy.

I was baptized into the Catholic church since that was the tradition of our faith. Though most Catholic families had their children baptized when they were babies, my parents decided to wait until I was older. I was assigned a couple by my parents, who would become my godparents. Their role was to take care of me in case I became an orphan.

My Godparents, Jose Sabates and Maria Belizon.

My godparents were *Jose Sabatés and Maria Belizon Sabates,* an older couple who were jewelers and had ten children. Even though Cuba was in chaos during Castro's regime, my godparents had the financial resources to sustain themselves, their families, and even their friends until they were able to leave the country.

I remember their warm and beautiful home. The house had an open courtyard in the middle of their house with tinajones, big round clay pots that held water. These were very resourceful in our city of Camaguey. Even though some memories of their home have faded, one thing will always remain: their love. Best of all was the welcoming feeling I received whenever we went to visit them.

Maria always gave me big squeezable hugs, which made me feel loved beyond measure. Jose was an impressive man, tall and larger than life in stature and character. He shared many words of wisdom when I went to visit him. He was strong and compassionate. His smile always brought a grin to my face. His knowledge of words always fascinated me. I loved being around him. He was a man of integrity, an upstanding citizen, honest and reliable, always there for his family and friends. My father considered him to be one of his closest and faithful friends whom he had known since they were young.

My godparents came to our rescue many times, including providing some financial means for us to get out of Cuba. The Sabatés are extraordinary people. I will never forget how they helped our family with their love and generosity.

There were many memories spent with loved ones, like a sunny day at a beach called Tarafa, where our family spent time with my godparents and their families.

Though I was young, I can still picture some of my godparents' grandchildren, like *Jose, Manty Sabatés, and Felix Sabatés Jr. (Chanito).* Felix became a prominent citizen, philanthropist, and a successful business owner in Charlotte, North Carolina. He was a NASCAR and IndyCar Team owner and one of the founding owners of the Charlotte Hornets basketball team.

I remember my father telling me the story of when Felix arrived in the United States, how he was able to put his past behind and never looked back.

With hard work and determination, Felix applied the principles of honesty, integrity, and always keeping his word, just like his father, Faliciano Sabates, and his grandparents.

For this reason, my father believed that God had richly blessed him in his accomplishments. Felix and his family did not allow the injustices of a communist regime to taint their future.

My father had always been close to the Sabates family. I remember some of my godparent's sons too. But the ones that stick out in my memory the most were *Mario,*

Guillermo, and Feliciano Sabatés. I looked forward to seeing when my dad would take me to their home. As a young child, I always felt loved by this family. But now it was time to say goodbye.

My cousin Eleana, my payaso (Clown), and me with a baby doll my aunt Emma gave me for Christmas.

The intrusion of the revolution short-lived my earliest memories of making friends. One of my fondest memories was of a family who had a daughter, whom I used to play with occasionally. Lourdes was a childhood friend who lived about a block from my house. Even though I wasn't allowed to see her often, I still remember her fondly.

One day my dad told me he was going to take me to visit Lourdes. As we knocked on Lourdes's door, her mother opened it and said, "Please, come in, but be very quiet. Helenita, Lourdes can no longer play with you as she used to because she is terribly ill!"

I looked at her perplexed, not understanding what she meant until I walked into Lourdes's room. She was bedridden. She had contracted polio, and it had paralyzed both

Alicia my cousin, who I never saw again after I left Cuba.

her legs.

My heart sank, but I pretended not to notice, if that was even possible. Lourdes's mother assisted her in her wheelchair, and that day we played with her baby dolls. After a brief visit, my father and I left.

A few days later, my father and I were taking a walk a few blocks from our home. As we passed by Lourdes's house, my father suddenly stopped. When my father realized that there was a note on her door, he rapidly tried to whisk me away. Unfortunately, it was too late, and I saw the official yellow piece of paper sealing shut Lourdes' home. I did not understand what happened to Lourdes and her family. I only saw her once again when we stayed at the Hotel Nacional in Havana. She was being wheeled into their room by her father. No one spoke a word, and I never saw her again.

Then there was my Aunt Isela, another one of my father's sisters. She was one of my favorite aunts on my father's side. She had jet black hair, and her eyes radiated pure love for friends and family. Her voice was always soft and pleasant. She had a beautiful laugh that was contagious. I always would break into a giggle when I heard her laugh. She used to call me "Chinita Poblana," which meant little China, village girl. It was a term of endearment.

I didn't necessarily say goodbye to all my family and friends; I went and visited them, thinking that I may see them again someday. However, I found out soon enough that these were some of the people that would eventually become a faraway memory of my past.

As the months passed, relatives, friends, and neighbors began to disappear. Eventually some of them emerged from prison detailing the accounts of cruelty they had endured.

However, some never reappeared, their lives cut short by deportation or executions for crimes they didn't commit.

We were living in a new world. The government expected us to adjust to their communist ways, without questioning their cruel intentions.

First picture is my mom, me on the slide, Jose at the top of the slide & Felix Sabates (Chanito).

DIVINE INTERVENTION

Chapter 21

At the Rotary Club in Camaguey. My dad is in front. My godfather, Jose Sabates, is 6th from the left on the long table.

Our family followed the latest reports as the media continued to deliver more disturbing news. A sense of bitter disgust became the new plague.

One day in April 1962, while my parents and I were sitting at the table eating some tropical fruits, there was a knock on our door. My mother said, "Helenita, go and answer the door but be careful." I got up from my chair and went to open the front door. It was the postman. He was standing outside with his bag slung over his shoulder with a grin on his face. He was holding out a long manila envelope. "All for you. I hope it's what you all have been waiting for!" said the mailman.

I took it and thanked him before closing the door. I ran to my dad and handed him the envelope.

After months of waiting, my parents finally received the approved visa waiver immigration papers, which permitted us to leave our island. We will be forever grateful to my father's friend, *Comellas*, who worked for Pan American Airways. He was able to speed up the process of our legal papers. We were all surprised and happy at the same time.

I was now approximately a month away from turning eight years old. It was April 10, 1962. The heat and mugginess offered no comfort. On this date, Guillermo Sabatés, one of my godparent's sons, drove us to the beautiful city of Havana, nearly two-hundred miles from Camaguey.

When we arrived, my father booked us a room at the Hotel Nacional, a very exquisite hotel by Cuban standards.

While in Havana my parents and I reminisced of times spent strolling on the Paseo—formerly known as the Prado. It ran from the center of Havana to the seawall.

The Morro Castle Fort, at the entrance of Havana harbor, was built in the late sixteenth century as a protection against buccaneers. However, later it was called La Cabaña.

The government had turned it into a prison for the so-called enemies of the revolution, where Che Guevara was responsible for hundreds of executions.

The next day, April 11, 1962, Guillermo drove us to the airport, hoping they would let us leave the country. Since flights out of Cuba were irregular at best, Guillermo wanted to make sure that if anything went wrong, he could drive us back to Camaguey.

Gratitude is not a big enough word to describe the gesture Guillermo extended to our family. I will forever be grateful for his kindness and willingness to help us, risking his own life to protect ours.

When we arrived at the airport, we waited for our papers to be approved. My stomach was in knots, not knowing what could happen if they turned us away.

I kept sensing that something unexpected was about to occur. However, despite the mixed emotions and confusion I was feeling, I knew that I had to be strong, if not for myself but for my parents.

Though I was a child in stature, my mind began to change, and something deep inside of me shifted into thinking like an adult.

As we stood waiting for our papers to be approved, I remember wearing several coats and holding my small suitcase.

Even at the airport, the rebels would demand anything of value that we had in our possession. My parents wanted to make sure that when we got to America, we would have a little something of value to survive on. For this reason, my mother had hidden some jewelry in my socks that my godparents had given us for our journey. I also held a couple of gold rings in my mouth. The rings were small, but they were still uncomfortable, and they were irritating my gums. I couldn't help worrying that I may accidentally swallow one ofthem.

While no one was looking, I managed to take my rings out of my mouth and snuck them in my socks with the others.

My parents knew that even as we stood in line to board a plane for the United States, there were still no guarantees we would be allowed to leave the island. Castro's men changed the rules for emigration every day.

Another one of my father's cousins was a young lawyer who had applied for permission to leave the country with his wife and two daughters. The government allowed him to leave with the promise that his family would join him shortly in New York. Hector told his family he would get a job so that he could provide for them when they arrived in the United States.

Hector worked hard, sending money back to Cuba. Each time, the government required more and more payment in exchange for his family's freedom. The Cuban government never kept their promises, and his wife and daughters were never allowed to leave.

Hector fell in a desperate state of depression for not being able to reunite with his family. After several years, he was unable to endure the separation from his wife and children, and he committed suicide.

Many families were separated because of unkept promises made by the Cuban government. The sad truth was that some fathers, mothers, children, husbands, wives, and other relatives never saw their families ever again after leaving the island.

As we stood at the gate waiting for the signal to board the plane, something went terribly wrong. A tall *miliciano* (militant) carrying a machine gun stepped into my father's path.

The man looked like a giant to me. My father asked him what the problem was, and he told my father, "*Callese!*" (Shut up!). When my father stated that we had all the necessary legal papers to leave, the man replied, "You and your family will not leave today!"

Hearing this man tell my father to shut up almost brought me to tears. My father had been a well-respected born citizen of our country, who ensured that as a journalist and newscaster he would bring the truth to his people.

Now he was being talked down to, disrespected, and humiliated. I so much wanted to hug him and tell him that everything was going to be alright. I hated to see him this way.

The thought of going back to our hometown frightened me. Rumors of people who had been denied exit out of Cuba were reported, stoned, beaten, and ridiculed when they had to return to their hometown. Now we were stamped and labeled traitors of the revolution.

The Urban Reform of our city had given orders to the G-2 headquarters to detain us at the airport for anti-communist activities.

My father was taken to their office and interrogated by the rebels.

While the interrogation was in process, my father said, "Sir, you've seen all our papers, but this individual at the gate insisted that we could not leave the country!"

"I'm sorry, but you, your wife, and your daughter must return to your city of Camaguey," the rebel replied.

The look on my father's face slowly diminished to sadness. He knew that if he said another word, he might jeopardize us leaving the country for good. He kept silent.

At that moment, my father took my mother's hand, held mine, and began to walk away, to face our impending danger.

Suddenly, my mother did the unexpected! She had always been a good wife, still tending to my father's needs in excess. Not because he might have deserved it or she had to, but because she loved him so much.

Every day she would take off my father's shoes when he would come home from a tiring day at work and put his bedroom slippers on. She would always make sure that his tie would be perfectly straight. She believed that the way my father looked to others reflected how she treated him and cared for him.

But on this day, she must have proposed that it was going to be different.

For the first time in their married life, she let go of my father's lead. Without giving it a second thought that my dad might have stopped her, she pulled away from my father's grip and took me back to the gate. By the time we got to the gate, there had been a change of rebels. The one standing there now seemed to be less intimidating. Without hesitation, my mother pleaded, "Please let our daughter board the plane!"

I didn't know what to think. From seeing my parents

living a comfortable life in our humble home—to watching my parents crawling on the floor to keep me safe from flying bullets outside my window—to now watching my mother begging for me to be set free. My father froze as he watched his wife pleading with the rebel.

In the meantime, my father had a boost of boldness after seeing my mother's courage. Again, he, too, decided to go back into the interrogation room, knowing he would be taking a big risk. However, when he entered the office again, the rebel that greeted him had an unusual quiet countenance.

Though he was with the revolution, he had a kindness that did not quite fit with what he stood for. He took a chance and asked him if I could board the plane. The rebel asked my father if he had documents for me, and my father replied, "Yes."

The rebel put his hand on my father's shoulder and said, "If you have the documents for your daughter, she can board the plane right now." He continued, "I'll take full responsibility for her departure." My father told me that it was a sincere gesture of kindness and risk on the part of this man.

Before going through the gate, I looked at my parents one last time. As always, I ran to my father first. My bond with him was indescribable. He leaned down and, with open arms, embraced me. I smiled up at him, hoping my smile would show, instead of my sadness.

To me, my father was the most stunning man I had ever seen or known. Words cannot explain how much I loved him. But now all I could see was a broken man.

Because of the painful decision of having to let me go, at

that moment, I was afraid that my father might cry, something I had never seen him do. Instead, he smiled, but I knew he was sad. He then held me tight once more and kissed me goodbye.

My mother, on the other hand, knelt to my level and reminded me to be good. She said, "Helenita, don't cry; we will be together again. God will help us, you'll see!"

They searched me at the gate without finding anything to confiscate. Then the rebel opened the gate and waved me through, as if the unseen hand of an angel was guiding the rebel's every move.

I looked back at my parents, hoping that by some miracle, they would let them come with me too, but something in my gut told me that it was not to be so.

There was also a group of children waiting to board the plane by themselves. Some were crying, and others didn't want to let go of their parents. What a sad picture that was!

They were called the Pedro Pan, or Peter Pan. Sadly, for many of these children boarding the plane by themselves, it meant that they would never return home or see their parents, families, or friends ever again.

The exodus of children sent to the United States began between 1960 and 1962. Approximately fourteen thousand unaccompanied minors left Cuba, leaving their families behind. These children left Cuba, not knowing what kind of life awaited them ninety miles away from their loved ones.

My mother had struck up a conversation with a lady named Consuelo before I was permitted to board the plane. She asked Consuelo if she would look after me on the flight until I reached Miami.

My mother trusted this stranger, though she had no idea who she was; however, there was no other choice but to trust God that I would be safe.

My parents had realized that they had to do whatever it took to send me to the United States. My father said to me later in life, "Helenita, your exit out of Cuba happened because *Gods' divine intervention* was in place."

To say that I was terrified of what awaited me on the other side of the ocean is an understatement.

I took a deep breath and tried to stay calm, but fear of the unknown was ever-present. It was frightening to leave all I knew, but things had moved quickly after the Revolution, and we had no other choice than to seek help from the United States.

Who would have known that my parents' difficult decision of sending me to America would change the course of my life forever!

With a mixture of relief and disbelief, I walked up the stairs of the airplane. I could still hear my mother shouting, "When you get to Miami, look for your Aunt Emma and your cousins! We love you!"

As I sat down by the window next to the lady my mother had entrusted to look after me, I stared outside the little window of the plane, wondering what had just happened. With tears streaming down my cheeks, feeling a lump in my throat, I continued to wave goodbye to my parents, until the airplane went around a curve and they were out of my view. All I could think of now was, *Would I ever see my parents again? Would I ever see my country again?*

COMING TO AMERICA

Chapter 22

As the plane descended, I felt a sudden rush in my head and a sick, dizzy feeling in my stomach. When I arrived in Miami, I lost track of the lady my mother had entrusted to watch over me. There was a group of men and women waiting for us, but I had no idea who they were. Two ladies took me and placed me with a group of children. They directed me toward a bus line and told us they were taking us to a camp for displaced children. These were places run by *Catholic charities* trying to help the many thousands of children that came in the Pedro Pan exodus.

IN MIAMI

I remember feeling bewildered and utterly confused about what had just happened. I couldn't wrap my brain around the fact that I was all alone in this big airport full of people I didn't even know—that just a few hours ago, I was in Cuba with my parents. However, I was about to experience my new life of freedom.

I laid down my little suitcase and took off my coat. The temperature was blistering hot, and I broke out in a sweat. I looked nervously around the airport at the other travelers. I had no idea of what I was supposed to do next.

People around me spoke a language I didn't understand, giving me a frightening headache, but there was nothing I could do, hoping my aunt Emma would claim me soon. I began praying and asking God not only for protection but that I would find my aunt soon.

Then as I was almost boarding one of the buses, I heard my name being called, "Helenita! Helenita!"

It was my Aunt Emma and my cousins, Emmita and Mirtha, calling me from the crowd.

I turned away from the bus and ran towards them, giving no thought to the people in charge of making sure I got on the bus with the rest of the Pedro Pan children. I was so glad to see a familiar face. I loved my Aunt Emma and my two cousins. As I ran, I remembered all the splendid times we had in Cuba. Whenever I got in trouble with my mom, my aunt would stick up for me, like when one of my cousins, Mirtha, and I ventured into a forbidden, dangerous neighborhood.

It had rained the previous night, so that day the roads were very muddy. To get to the other side of the neighborhood, we had to go across a large mud puddle. Halfway through it, we realized that the mud hole was deeper and thicker than we thought. Struggling halfway through it, we fell in, sinking into this muddy water up to our waist. At that moment, we knew we were in trouble. After some effort trying to pull ourselves out of the mud, we hurried back home. We were unrecognizable.

When we finally got home, my other cousin, Emmita, hosed us down with the water hose. When our mothers got home, they quickly figured out that we had been up to no good.

Both of my cousins got in trouble and chased around with a *chancleta* (flip flop), but my aunt spoke up for me and made me the innocent victim. However, if you ask my cousins, they might have a different version of the story.

I also remembered my parents and I attending one of my cousin's heavenly programs at their school, *Las Salesianas*. They were both dressed up as angels.

They looked so angelic with those white robes, wings, and halos. Mirtha, with her cute dimples, could fool just about anybody. However, I knew her well enough to know that she was no angel.

But, on this day, I didn't care what kind of angels my cousins had been; I was just glad to see their familiar faces. When I reached them, I immediately embraced them; I didn't want to let them go.

For a long time, I did not know what happened to the countless Pedro Pan children that came on those flights. Much later in life, I found out that many of them ended up in camps, orphanages, or foster care. Later, some were reunited with their parents, but a lot of them never saw their parents again.

WITH MY COUSINS.

SURPRISE

Chapter 23

MY MOTHER AND I IN MIAMI. OUR LAST PICTURE TOGETHER.

I went to live in my aunt and uncle's apartment. Every evening I would sit at the foot of my bed in deep thought. I often wondered what my future would be in Miami without my parents. Often, I stared out my window, trying to identify all the new and different sounds and smells of this amazing city.

Though many times I felt empty inside for not being able to be in my own country with my parents, I was still grateful to be in America. I missed my parents so much. Days passed with no word from them. My aunt and uncle would say to me, "It won't be long, Helenita, they'll be here before you know it." It was a never-ending wait. In my mind, I just wasn't sure if I would ever see them again.

Every day I went to school with my cousins, working

on learning a new language. It all seemed so hard for me, not knowing the language. I couldn't focus on schoolwork. All I thought about was being with my parents.

It had only been a week since I left Cuba, but it seemed like it had been months. Since my arrival in Miami, I had prayed every night for my parents to join me. However, the days came and went, and I heard no news from them.

I was discouraged and depressed; I didn't have the drive to do anything. Every night, I cried myself to sleep.

On *Thursday, April 19, 1962,* while I was sitting in the living room with my cousins, I heard the front door open —in walked both of my parents. I am not sure which one was running faster, my heart or my legs, but I ran across the room and embraced them. All I could do was cry tears of joy as I held them tight.

I didn't want to let go, just in case it was a dream. But my parents were really there, hugging me and telling us the miraculous story of how they were allowed to leave the island.

After they saw me board the airplane to Miami, my father was arrested and interrogated further, concerning his betrayal to the revolution. At this point, my parents had no idea if they would ever see me again. After his release from jail, he and my mother had no choice but to go back to Camaguey.

Once my parents returned to their hometown, the people that once respected them now taunted them by yelling, "Guzano (worm) get out of Cuba, we don't want you here!"

My father was verbally attacked and continuously insulted with profanity and humiliating acts by the revolutionaries.

The Communists had demanded more money, property, or anything of value. My father said that the communists kept up their extortion, always wanting more, so my parents resorted to their very last option.

One of my mother's sisters, Hortensia, who was married to a prominent physician in Havana, came to their rescue. They were my parent's last resource to get out of Cuba.

My Aunt Hortensia and my Uncle Julio had one daughter, my cousin, Alicia. They generously provided money for my parents to give to the government so that they could leave the country. Eventually, my aunt and my cousin left Cuba and went to live in Sweden, but my uncle Julio never made it out of Cuba. After I left, I never saw them again.

With the help of our relatives, my parents again requested permission to leave the country, and they were granted permission. When they finally got to the airport, the same rebel who had stopped my father the first time did it again. My father said he just froze when he stood before him.

My father said to himself; *this could not be happening again.*

From the corner of his eye, he spotted another rebel. This time, it was the rebel that had been so kind to him when I boarded the plane by myself.

The rebel approached my dad and asked him if he had legal papers for my mother. My father said he did. The rebel told him that there was only one seat left in the plane, and he would allow my mother to board. He promised my dad that he could leave on the next afternoon flight, but my father didn't trust them.

My Uncle Dagoberto, one of my father's brothers, who had driven my parents to the airport, said to my dad, "This can't be happening! It's impossible, you have complied with all their wants and extortions!"

My dad answered, “Everything here is possible, my brother, this is what this revolution has done to us.”

At first, my mother refused to get on the plane. She cried, telling my dad, “Arnaldo, I will not leave you behind. We’ve been through so much together. I will not leave without you!”

But my dad would not have it.

He pulled away from my mother’s tight grip and said to her, “Get on that plane for our daughter’s sake, Helenita needs you, I will be fine, we will be together again.”

Though my father knew that the best thing for my mother was for her to get on that flight, he later told me his heart was desperately longing to hold her and keep her with him.

As he turned to walk away, he took one last glimpse at my mother and then turned and walked away.

Thinking that now he had to start from scratch and make a new living for himself; he said to my uncle, “Brother, I guess we will stay behind and fight for what is right. We will survive, just like when we were young and left as orphans. If I must sell coffee and make three cents per cup or sell roasted peanuts on the streets, I will start from zero, but I will do it in Havana.

I will never return to Camaguey, ever again. One day, our country will rise again, because no terrible thing can last one hundred years.

I consider myself more of a Cuban than these people who called themselves patriots. If my destiny is to stay here, I will fight to see the downfall of this communist regime."

At that moment, a miracle happened, one that changed my parent's lives. He heard his name being called on the intercom, "Attention, Arnaldo Cebrian! You must present yourself at the ticket counter, immediately!"

My father and his brother looked at each other in surprise and gasped. When my father reached the ticket counter, he spotted the rebel that had helped him before.

He said to my father, "We had a lady that had decided not to board the plane because her grandchildren were not allowed to travel with her. We told her to wait for the next flight since she refused to separate herself from her family."

The rebel asked my dad if he wanted the empty seat.

My father jumped with joy, saying, "Yes, yes, of course, I want the seat!"

The rebel said to my father before he boarded the plane, "You are a very lucky man for this to have happened!"

"No, sir, God has guided my footsteps!" My father replied.

My father told me that later he thought about the lady that gave up her seat. He felt bad because he knew one of the government's tactics was to separate the family. He was not too sure there would be any guarantees the lady and her grandchildren would ever leave the island, but he had faith. He felt that her sacrifice would reward her someday.

My father was not a religious man, but he had great faith that God's plan was the best plan for us. He said he knew now that the hand of the Almighty God had orchestrated everything that happened at the Havana airport.

As my father walked onto the plane, he spotted my sobbing mother. When he reached her, she jumped to her feet and melted into his arms. Still holding on to each other, they heard the stewardess's announcement, "Pan American Airlines is departing from Cuba to Miami, Florida. Everyone, please, take your seats and buckle up for take-off!"

My parents looked at each other and broke into laughter, something they hadn't done since the revolution had started in Cuba.

As their plane ascended toward the sky, my parents had only one thing in mind—*Freedom!*

***

There we were, the three of us, embracing each other. There would be no more need for whispers, no long lines to get food, and no more hiding from expressing our political and religious views. Here, we were together again in this great country. Completely free.

WORK AND SCHOOL IN AMERICA

Chapter 24

Tensions between the United States and the Soviet Union over Cuba increased since the failed Bay of Pigs invasion in 1961. The Cuban Missile Crisis came a year and a half later. A few months after I arrived in Miami, an American U-2 spy plane secretly photographed nuclear missile sites built by the Soviet Union on the island of Cuba. This brought the United States and the Soviet Union to the brink of nuclear conflict.

Nuclear warheads were now stationed ninety miles off the American coastline. Since no one was sure how the Soviet Leader, Nikita Khrushchev, would respond to the naval blockade and the United States' demands, everyone was on edge. Though our lives had been in danger many times in Cuba, now our very existence was threatened.

Fortunately, both superpowers recognized the devastating possibility of a nuclear war. Therefore, they agreed to a deal with the Soviets dismantling the weapon sites in exchange for a pledge from the United States not to invade Cuba.

Though it wasn't the intention of my parents, relatives,

and most of the Cuban population to pursue permanent residence here in the United States, we realized that returning to our country was no longer an option.

For this reason, my parents accepted that the United States would become our new homeland. Therefore, my parents began the initiative to improve our lives by working hard and providing for our family.

Coming to America was one of the best things that could have happened to us, as hard as it was at first.

My father's first job was selling fresh Cuban bread door-to-door. This job didn't pay enough for our necessary expenses, so he eventually found another job at the "Carillon" hotel in Miami Beach. He cleaned tables and washed dishes or whatever they asked him to do. Every night my father would come home from work, physically and mentally exhausted.

Having to wash the continuous dishes, glasses, cups, silverware, and more were no comparison to the life he led in Cuba. Though it was hard work, he tried to do it with joy and dignity. He knew he was blessed to have found this job in a country where he didn't speak their language. He never complained.

One day as my father was cleaning a table at his job, a man sitting nearby saw him and asked him in Spanish if he liked his job. My father replied, "Sir, I came from humble beginnings from Cuba. I worked extremely hard to have had everything taken from me and my family, by the communist regime, and I won't give up now. With God's help, I will work hard once again to achieve what the enemy stole from us." Armando Vidal, the founder of Continental Advertising, was so humbled by my father's answer, that he gave him a job at his company. My father worked for Armando for over twenty-five years.

My mother found a job in a factory assembling aluminum chairs. Later, she became a maid in a three-story hotel that had no elevator. With what my mother made, she no longer had the same privileges she once had in Cuba, but she never complained.

I remember my mother used to dress up for dinner. Her long slender hands, beautifully manicured, her nails shiny with a coat of light polish. She had exquisite jewelry. She would always wear her pearls as well as her intricate jade bracelet, one of her favorites. However, these were things of the past. She would always tell me, "Helenita, material things do not bring us happiness; they just make us comfortable, but it's not things that we need."

My mother never complained about the hard work she had to do in this country. Her doctor and our family warned her not to do heavy work, due to her heart condition, but she insisted. She would always tell us that we could not make ends meet with just my father's earnings.

While living with my aunt, I attended Highland Park Elementary School. My parents and I had moved several times, and I still was not able to speak English. My parents began to get concerned about my educational development.

After a year passed, my parents enrolled me at Gesu Catholic School. By now, I could only pick up a few English words here and there, but not much more.

Though I spent most of every Sunday tortured with a stomachache because Monday was too quickly approaching, I told no one about my ailments.

Every day when I entered my classroom, I would fear that I might not read well enough or understand the math or spell words the nuns would give me.

The unease I harbored in my stomach felt like a permanent resident. Everything made me anxious.

One day, Mother Theresa, my second-grade teacher, had told the class we had to do seatwork while she ran an errand. She left one of the other students to watch the classroom for her. When she left, I asked one of the students that spoke both English and Spanish to translate the seat work for me, but she wouldn't answer me. Of course, the student in charge wrote my name on the board for talking. I was still struggling with the English language, and I wanted to get my work done before Mother Theresa came back. However, no one would help in fear of getting in trouble with our nun.

When mother Theresa came back to the classroom and saw my name written on the blackboard, she came straight toward me. I panicked! Though I couldn't understand her, I had a feeling something bad was about to happen.

She grabbed me by the arm and stood me up from my seat. I tried to explain to her that I didn’t understand English and was trying to get some help, but of course, she didn't understand a word I was saying in Spanish.

Unfortunately, before I could try to explain myself further, she had what seemed like a meltdown.

She began to swing her old ruler on my bare legs, repeatedly, leaving long lash marks on both my legs! Tears rolled down my cheeks as my legs burned from the sting of the wooden ruler.

I never told my parents about the incident. I feared

they would come to my school and make a scene, making it worse for me. However, I did get something out of that traumatic experience. Though my early years of school in America were quite an experience because of the language barrier, I survived with blood, sweat, and tears. It is incredible what the human brain can learn under pressure.

Though I do not condone Mother Theresa's harsh behavior, it gave me the incentive to learn English quickly. I learned that this was the exception, not the rule, and I never held it against her.

I was now in the third grade and had survived second grade with Mother Theresa. My third-grade teacher, Mrs. McCrary, was not a nun. She was a firm but compassionate teacher, who understood the struggles that many Cuban children faced in a new culture. No matter how busy she was, she always took the time to help me and encourage me to do better. I eventually became a straight "A" student in her class.

AN UNEXPECTED LIFE

Chapter 25

After my parents had been working for a little while, they had saved enough money to buy us an old car that looked like it was from the 1940s. The body was long with a huge hatchback. It was an ugly gold, mustard-like color. I distinctly remember that the car made a lot of noise when you first turned the ignition. The first time we took a ride in this old but convenient car, the exhaust pipe let out what sounded like a gunshot—we all ducked down instinctively. The brief moment of happiness and safety, broken by the unforgettable bad memories of the chaos my family and I experienced in Communist Cuba. We quickly realized it was just our car letting us know that he was an old wore out piece of metal that needed some tender loving care. After that brief scare, we all laughed out loud. We realized that here in America, the likelihood of gunshots flying through your car for no apparent reason was more of the exception than the rule.

My health was still not improving, and I continued with respiratory problems. Twice a week, my mother would take me to the doctor for treatments at the Freedom Tower. There were times when she was too weak even to make it out the door, but she always put my medical needs before hers.

The Freedom Tower was the Miami Cuban Refugee Emergency Center. It became the focal point of refugee registration assistance, relief, and resettlement. They offered us free basic medical care and some financial help until my parents were able to get on their feet and provide for our family.

Each week we were blessed with a shoebox full of goodies. There was usually a block of cheese, Spam, toiletries, cookies, and even a small toy for me. I still remember the sweet aroma that came from the combination of the cheese and the cookies in that box—I would still recognize it to this day.

I'll never forget the first time my parents took me to a grocery store. After those years of rationed food in Cuba, I was amazed at how much food was available to us here in the states. It was such an intriguing feeling that we now had the freedom to buy whatever we wanted as long as we had money.

One day my parents decided to surprise me by taking me to a popular place called Burger King. They told me they had saved a little bit of money to treat ourselves to whatever we wanted to eat. I was beside myself. I ordered the biggest sandwich they had, the *Whopper*. I had never tasted anything so good in my life. I was eating it so fast that my mother had to tell me to slow down, but I couldn't stop savoring it.

After we finished eating at Burger King, we went to visit one of my second cousins on my father's side, Mercy. She was the cutest little toddler I had ever seen. She always reminded me of Shirley Temple with her curly hair. Her parents had invited us over to eat.

Though we had already eaten, we accepted their invitation.

When we got to their house, Mercy's mom asked me if I was still hungry. Though I was full to the brim, I said yes. So that day, I had my first *Whopper* and my first steak within an hour of each other. Boy, was I hungry!

Two years after being in the United States, I was finally able to speak English well. One night, my mother called me into her bedroom. She said she wanted to talk with me. She began to tell me about the importance of being obedient. She seemed very worried, but I couldn't figure out why.

I remember the conversation as if it were yesterday. I laid down on my mother's bed beside her. She began to tell me things that may happen in the future. Her message sounded urgent as if time was of the essence.

As I listened to her, I began to get concerned. She said, "Helenita, I want you to know that if anything ever happens to me, and I end up in the hospital, I need you to tell the doctors to save my life, no matter the cost! Now that you can speak English, you can translate between your dad and the doctors."

Having grown up knowing of her delicate heart condition, I began to cry uncontrollably. She continued, "You see, Helenita, if I die, you will have a very rough life. Your dad might remarry, and your stepmom might not treat you right or might not even want you!" With trembling lips, I said, "Mom, why are you saying that?" There was only silence. I rocked my body back and forth, tears trailing one after another down my face. My hands shook as I reached up and wiped them away.

When my mother and her siblings were left orphaned,

their experience growing up with their grandfather was very dysfunctional and abusive. So, it goes to reason that she didn't want the same thing to happen to me. Of course, as a child I was not aware of what she had gone through in her own personal life.

After that conversation, my mother said, "Helenita, everything is going to be alright. I just wanted to prepare you if something were to happen to me; so you would know what to do." I fell asleep in her arms. I didn't want to think about what she had just told me anymore.

The next day was like any other day. After school, my mother took me to the clinic for my weekly respiratory treatments. After three hours of waiting and having treatments, we took the bus home.

My mother and I got off the bus and started walking towards the house. Suddenly, my mother stopped. She said, "Helenita, my legs feel like lead; they feel so heavy." I helped her walk a little way on the sidewalk, but she told me she couldn't walk anymore.

I was now almost eleven years old, and the thought of her conversation with me the previous night flooded my mind. Then in a panic, I heard her say, "Helenita, run and get some help!"

I was torn between leaving her by herself and running to get her some help. However, she insisted that I go. I ran as fast as I could. When I got home, I rushed in and got my two cousins, Emmita and Mirtha.

When my cousins and I got to my mother, we found her sitting on the hot pavement. She was still conscious but very weak. Between the three of us, we helped her up and walked her slowly to the house.

One of my cousins called my aunt, and my dad at work, and they rushed home. By now, my mother was throwing up and having chest pains. My father insisted on calling an ambulance, but she kept begging them not to take her to the hospital. My father convinced her anyway.

When the ambulance arrived and put her on the stretcher, she glanced at me with anguish, reminding me of her conversation with me. The ambulance sounded the siren, even though she had asked them not to. They took her to Jackson Memorial Hospital. That was April 27, 1964.

On April 28, 1964, my dad and I went to see my mother at the hospital. She looked so pale, but still so beautiful. I sat beside her on the hospital bed and reminded her that I would tell the doctors to do whatever it cost to save her life, just like she had told me.

Later that evening, my aunt came and picked me up from the hospital while my dad stayed with my mother. I gave my mother a hug, and kissed her goodbye, thinking I would see her again the next day. With her stunning green eyes, she waved at me and smiled.

On April 29, I left school around 4:30 in the afternoon. As I waited for the city bus, I started thinking of how I could get a ride to the hospital to see my mother again. I asked people around the bus stop if they knew which bus would take me to Jackson Memorial Hospital. Some of them nodded their heads, "No!" Others warned me that it wasn't a very good neighborhood. They said that no one should be around that area this late in the day, especially a young child like me.

I finally decided not to go and just took the bus home.

As soon as I got home, I went upstairs to my room, changed my uniform, and cleaned my black and white shoes, as I did every day.

While looking at myself in the mirror of an old wooden dresser in my bedroom, I had this childish thought come to my mind.

I grabbed a rusty bobby pin and began carving my mother's name alongside mine. I told myself, *If anything happens to my mother, I will always have her memory right here.*

Suddenly, my daydreaming was interrupted by what sounded like screaming and crying. It was coming from downstairs. I didn't give it much thought since my cousins sometimes would fight over silly stuff as most siblings do.

I carefully grabbed the school shoes that I had finished cleaning with the usual white chalky liquid so I wouldn't get it on my clothes. However, before I took another step down the stairs, my cousin Emmita stopped me and said, "Helenita, don't cry, but your mom just died!" I can't imagine how hard it was for my cousin to deliver those devastating words. My cousins adored my mom, and now she was gone. Until this day, that moment remains etched in my memory.

The shock of those words kept pounding in my head like a drum. When I said goodbye to my mother the previous night at the hospital, I had no idea that it would be the last time I would see her alive.

I dropped the shoes I was holding in my hands and screamed as I ran hysterically outside towards our neighbor's house. My cousins were crying and yelling my name, "Stop, Helenita, stop!" But like a blind child, I ran without seeing where I was going.

When I reached my neighbor's house, I banged on her door until she opened it. I continued to scream, saying, "My mom is dead! My mom is dead!" Somehow, I was trying to convince myself that all this was a dream.

This poor woman, who was Hungarian, couldn't understand a word I was saying, but she wrapped her arms around me and whispered soft Hungarian words that somehow soothed me.

There was a popular song playing on the radio at our house that day called *Going to the Chapel.* To this day, when I hear this song, it takes me back to the day my mother died.

I progressed from screaming and crying to complete silence. There were so many thoughts and feelings going through my mind on that awful day. I was scared of my mother's reminder of what my future awaited me. I was overcome with guilt because I didn't have the opportunity to tell the doctors to save her life, as I had promised her. *What if I had been there and done what she had asked me? Would she still be alive today?* The same questions haunted me for many years after her death, but eventually, I blocked anything that had to do with my mother's memory.

As my father prepared for my mother's funeral, I pretended that she was on a long trip. I didn't want to hear anything about the funeral or the burial. However, my father insisted I attend the viewing so I could have some closure.

While at the funeral home, my father gently pushed me towards the casket, where my mother rested peacefully. My knees buckled at the sight of her lifeless body. An indescribable pain in my heart would not leave me. She didn't look like herself.

I wanted to remember my mother as the beautiful woman she was, with her beautiful blonde hair and her striking green eyes.

At my request, my father had a Cuban flag made of carnations on top of her casket. I wanted it to remind me of the good memories we had on our island when I was young.

I've never forgotten the sacrifices my mother made, alongside my father, always to protect me, even risking their own lives.

Years later, my father told me the story of what happened on April 29,1964, on the day before my mother's forty-first birthday.

While at the hospital, the doctors felt that a cardiac catheterization would be the right procedure to determine if they could repair her heart condition.

Since my parents didn't speak English, they were not sure what was going on. There were no interpreters available at the time. The language barrier limited my family from being proactive in deciding to either go ahead with the procedure or find an alternative.

As my father saw them wheeling my mother into another room, he desperately ran towards her to find out what the doctors were about to do.

In anguish, he held her hand, longing to save her. He was trying so hard to be strong for her, as she begged him not to let her go through this.

My father tried to communicate with the doctors, with a few English words he had learned, but no one could understand him. After the nurse placed my mother onto another gurney, they began to push it faster and faster. Soon she was wheeled through big metal doors, down a long hallway, with my father running alongside her. As their hands slipped away from each other, my father said he saw a tear fall softly down her cheeks. Before she was out of his view, he yelled from across the hallway, "I'll always love you, Sarah, you will always be my love!"

My father went into the chapel that was right next to the procedure room to pray. He could hear her scream in a panic for the doctors to stop doing whatever they were doing. There had not been any legal papers signed to perform the procedure, and if they had signed anything, they had no clue what they were signing, since the papers were written in English.

Then, suddenly there was an eerie silence in the chapel. My father told me that the only thing he could hear was the thumping of his own heart.

After my father walked out of the chapel, he saw my mother's doctor approach him. The doctor told him that her heart was too weak to tolerate the procedure and that she suffered a heart attack before they could even finish the test. My father buried his face in his hands and sobbed.

My father and my aunt felt trapped, as if in the twilight zone, unable to communicate their needs to anyone. My mother had lived for so long with this disease that our family could not believe she was dead.

Even the doctors they had visited years ago in the United States had told them that she would not have any problems living a reasonably healthy life with the new technology in medicine.

My father's life was never the same. He had many women he dated or cared about after my mother's death, but he told me that no other woman could ever occupy that place in his heart as my mother did.

***

Though no one knew how long my mother would have lived with her congenital heart disease, my father often wondered if she would still be alive, if only Fidel Castro had not changed the course of our lives. We will never know the answer to those daunting questions.

HE ADJUSTED OUR SAIL

Chapter 26

After my mother's death, life took me through a path I would have never chosen. However, without my experiences I would have never had the strength to make it this far.

For years I had tried to forget the memories of my past when I was uprooted from my homeland. Forgetting would have meant that the many Cubans placed in front of El Paredon and executed by a firing squad never existed. That those like my second cousin, Luisito, who was also executed for speaking against Communism, was not a reality.

For years I had shut my memory off from what our family went through during Castro's revolution. As I got older, my conscience would not allow me to forget. The many men, women, and children who died in the shark-infested waters trying to escape, is a truth I cannot deny.

Castro's Socialist, totalitarian regime denied us our most basic rights of freedom of speech and religion. Yes, forgetting would mean that all the good memories with my family and friends from my early childhood would have never existed.

Communism came crashing down on us, like a vast tidal wave, bringing us a substantial deal of sorrow and disappointment. However, we chose not to drown in our own pity. As the wind tried to toss us out of our country, God adjusted our sail, and landed us in the land of freedom, The United States of America.

This country has fed me, schooled me, clothed me, and sheltered me when I had none. It has given us equal opportunity.

Words cannot express enough how grateful I am to this country for allowing my family and me the freedom this democracy has offered us. Here, the most basic human rights are respected, giving us the hope of a better future. This country made a humane gesture, extending the hand of friendship to us, the Cuban people—helping us to break the chains that once held us captive by an oppressive government.

Because of this great detour in our lives, I believe God made us all winners and deeper human beings. We became heroes because we were able to sustain the force of the storms by anchoring our lives in our faith.

By the grace of God, we were able to navigate adversity by using the tools of hope. The evils that once intended to destroy us made us much stronger than we could have ever imagined.

My life is a simple one. I didn't become a well-known professor, a doctor, or a Harvard student. Instead, I faced many struggles in exile that could have finished me off. Through the years of many mistakes and bad choices, I learned not to allow the obstacles and failures of my past determine the future I was created to live.

I am blessed with a wonderful husband of 36 years and counting. We have two wonderful children that are wed to amazing spouses. And we are the proud grandparents of two grandsons and counting, who are and will always be the treasures that fill our hearts.

Faced with great difficulty and pain, I overcame the powerful lures of this world. God never left my side. When I was too weak to go on, He carried me through the trenches, but that is another story.

On November 3, 1976, when I was twenty-one, my father and I became American citizens. This experience was an honor for both of us. I am proud to be a Cuban American. I am beyond blessed.

My dad and I in front of an apartment building after the death of my mother.

ACKNOWLEDGEMENTS

It would have been impossible to have gotten this book into the world without the encouragement, direction, and love of family and friends. I want to start by thanking my amazing husband, for all the long nights and days I spent writing draft after draft for so many years. His patience with me is indescribable. Thank you for loving all of me.

I'm thankful to our children, who have heard me tell my stories a thousand times and never complained or seemed disinterested. My deepest thanks to my dear friend and constant support, Judy Clossin, who stayed up with me editing and rewriting my story for years, always saying, "You just have to finish this book!" She was my biggest cheerleader.

A big thank you to my friend, Amy Johnson, who fixed the torrential amounts of grammatical errors and challenged me in learning grammar through my writing. I'm also grateful to have had the opportunity of knowing Elizabeth Pease, who, with her artistic and brilliant mind, designed the cover of my book. She captured the very essence of how God's amazing light rescued my life. I want to thank my niece, Dani Kemper, who took the time to edit my manuscript, despite her busy schedule.

Thank you to Dr. Felix N. Sabatès, MD, for permission to use photos from his book, *From Cuba with a Vision*. I also want to thank my godparents, Jose Sabatés and Maria Belizon for helping us get out of Cuba. Also, my Uncle Julio and my Aunt Hortensia that made it possible for my parents to eventually exile to the United States.

To the many people who have helped me throughout the years in writing my story, I'm forever grateful. Thank you, Bobbie Jefferson, for your constant encouragement. Thank you, Sandy Fowler, for your part in editing the manuscript. I also want to thank the many friends who helped me write my story early on. Brenda Lowe, whose creativity helped me express my voice through my writing. Faith Markle, whom I met while living in North Carolina. She was the first person who edited and proofread my first manuscript. Thank you for your friendship. Caleb Wygal, my editor, publisher, and everything in between, thank you for answering my call to bring my story to fruition.

Although I'm sure I've left some names out, please know that I'm thankful for you. To those who gave heart and soul through prayer, words cannot express my gratitude.

To Cuba, my homeland that I dearly love, may I see the day of true liberation of our people.

Last but not least, I thank my heavenly Father for setting me free, indeed!

Made in USA - Kendallville, IN
1162731_9798667924937
10.22.2020 1648